MIND CHIMES

from

THESE TIMES

C. C. Aningo

Email: ccaningoboox@gmail.com
Blogsite: www.beamnaijadream.com

Dedication

To you, dear reader,
I hope you have some good conversations
with the voices you will hear.
Your focused company
is appreciated.
Thank you.
And equally
to my family and true friends.

Chukwuajalike

Contents

SYNERGY

Open the cage, preened pigeons fly
whichever direction.
Breathless, bloodless hands on
production lines—goods,
exact same definitions.
Poet here   engineer there—
handshake,   want to pair.
It's an altar, a shrine, a
marketplace, incubator;
they'll find
bunkers, bunk beds,
oxygen, pace and say
It's okay!

VPR ORATION

Ouch, that slap! Sharp cry I serve up; mouths erstwhile dry,
salivate, cheer. Something dear happened.

Right off, I imagine this world weird.

Main man; forehead beaded—sweat droplets; nose-mouth masked;
eyeballs enlarged—thick lenses.

I eavesdropped so long, I remember—
every language, every dialect, every spin number.
Ah pre-**VPR** genes hoard, talk!

Main man—gruff voice gruffer; ennui of routine.
They believe I can't smell, taste, hear, see, or feel—on that they bet.
Something they know not—gift I'll reveal not yet.

Main man's hands—sturdy, sculpted—Muhammad Ali, sumo
wrestler, no!
Weightlifter better, but bulging tummy obstructs.

My lungs push my chest, helium into airship—
strange sensation, strange connection.

They surround me, eyes dazed; I gaze at space panorama—stars blink
in haze.

My memory cache will make each one blush, grimace,
even think forensic note—conscience pace.

Failed nutrients, growth-rates' managers to me they rate.

Well, I better start early, learn mending fences.

Main man's biceps; those syringes, forceps, knives;
those gadgets wired or tubed to machines with screens: crawlers,
wigglers, spikers, winkers, chameleons on screens.
Many, many miracles are possible.

A minimalist supreme I've been; senseless clutter everywhere
in
extreme, Oh LORD of Lords!

Many moulting oats before My Lords, Your Honours, these days—
great freedom; great liberation; another kingdom.

I dodged magnetism's flux. I coiled up, slid around.
Diver off springboard—rolls. No bios for free, or cajoles, or
promises empty—the bios include my nudity!

That far corner one; so thin bones about to burst out—pickled, fried,
or boiled
cut from ribs slab.

Maybe I listened to too much ballyhoo; the oneness-
evenness bits, despite
assortment planks—allure! How frank?

Frazzled and razzled, there's more and more fantasy;
many misalignments dazzle, rattle agreements everywhere.
Convention sashays, poor thing.

Ah Goodness! They probe universe deeper;
probability discounted, unmathematical—great introductions;
great spin-offs; great fallouts, all radical. If emigration is it,
how will passenger manifests come about?
	Holdings hand out privilege permits;
	meaner, the remits.

Doctor Nduka has been on for years many; a favourite name in
homes aplenty.
	I never met or heard of him.

	My memory cache is not for cash; rampant massive spasms
	will
	lead total closures.

That one next to main man; tracks of flesh in stretched skin hang—
ridges across inclined
farm patch.

	I lived alone; no kin kicks in the face.

They know civilisations flourish, absorb the absurd, then perish.
	Maybe, they'll pelletise the globe.

	I was the utmost—everything catered for me.
	Now, I have to imbibe civilisation.

That near corner one: beard, moustache shaved to skin, legs too.
Heavyset frame; long fingernails; hips wriggle, sway; sonorous voice;
dashes of sweet perfumes—all have me troubled.

	I've been an optimisation specialist—not a bit more or less
	than needed.

The reticent, nervous one in the middle: her naked cousin raised eyebrows, energised neighbourhood eyes. Finally, he was doing it to a park tree slit. Respondents pulled
him off—wood splinters as darts! Blood drops smear, coagulate.

"All things living need love too; those people I always hear say it's true," he repeated—
euphoria, his face; no pain at hypersensitive dangler.

From the most exalted speakers, I heard it often—
ONE HUMANITY, ONE DESTINY.

That near corner again: rounded rears protrude, large belly overhangs. Preferences,
more fluid, freer these days.
Count me out to intrude; I'm still a prude, I swear.

Doctor Nduka, he's main man. He's shifting on his feet—is he holding back a long, loud,
rear-end, monotone fluting?
He knows better—eat proper.

Maybe, I should point my **VPR** to the near corner—some intelligent conversations.

The "P" word in my **VPR** sets them off in many ways.

My **VPR** served me well. I signalled and got whatever my need with my head, rump, feet, elbows, knees, body configurations.

Surprised them on arrival—
I am a girl not the boy expected, thanks to kits of my
Virtual Penetrating Rays.
Make a face or laugh; I can see and hear you—my **VPR**!

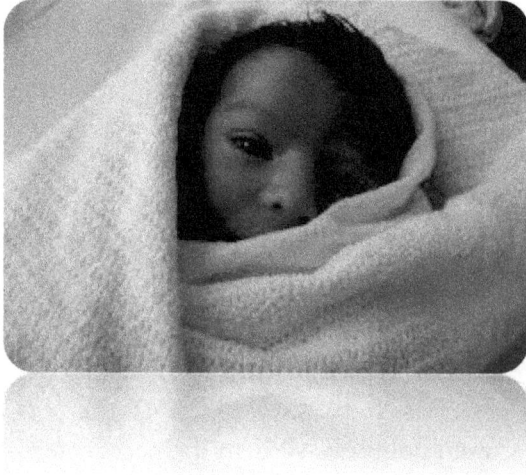

COURSE CORRECTION

I don't fully understand what now goes on,
but metronome ticks on, I must persist.
Marble chips of old to match future chips.
Why do both chip sets fail to click in?

As metronome ticks on and I persist,
crimson clouds cast sunlight, fear's halos.
Why do both chip sets fail to click in?
Their tongues and grooves are good fits.

For crimson clouds to cast sunlight, fear's halos,
strong actors make chip sets not click in;
their tongues and grooves are good fits.
Explosive atmosphere everywhere, ignitable.

Strong actors make chip sets not click in—
chip sets' makeups, their shelf lives.
With atmosphere everywhere so ignitable,
chip sets' interferences need careful repair.

From chip sets' makeups and shelf lives,
expansion coefficients cause interference.
Chip sets' interferences need careful repair;
hardness, temperatures call attention.

Expansion coefficients introduce interference;
marble grinder must hum and sparks not fly.
Hardness, temperature issues
worked on by work environment.

If marble grinder hums and sparks don't fly,
and marble chips of old match future chips,
with all actors tamed by work environment,
I'll begin to understand what now goes on.

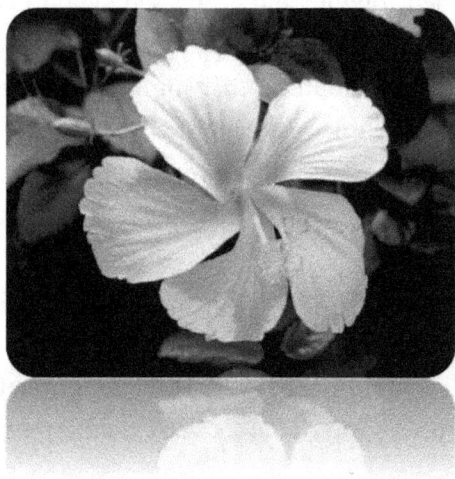

THE NATION DECIDES

We worsen fissures, fractures, divides.
Fissures widen; fractures deepen;
divides devise higher sides.
The nation, we then say, decides.

Old and young line up, vote.
Besides images that drift on,
what decision is truly won
that every side would serve and promote?

Democracy, democracy . . .
Many feisty fruit cocktails you dress.

STORMS GATHER

Pooled,
LAW for the ruled
for
rule of law
grows
sharp claws—
outlaws
claw hammer faults,
empty vaults.
Never
a one-off
nor
a run-off.

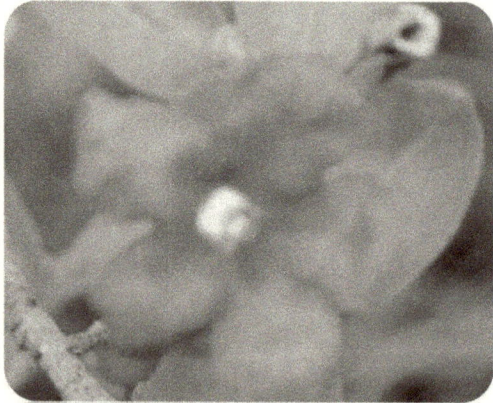

THE DANCE STOPS

Law court—the place for justice.
rich one, poor one, both remiss;
rich one winks perks for fees,
poor one shakes, pleads, pees.
By twists, side-by-side they lie at hospice.

EMPTY GESTURES

Warders betoken
The long broken
The just-now broken
The about-to-be broken
The fear of being broken
All have spoken
Prison camp is correction token

ALBATROSS

Brutes rule these days.
Poisonous carrots murderous sticks
leave dreams unfulfilled,
egalitarian and friends out of pace.
Life becomes chains of unkind picks;
pristine drives harpooned, never refilled.

Brutes rule these days.
Cold-blooded cabal—mean, usurpers vile,
induce in the land growth delays.
Bogus sales, common fortune stolen—
their trademarks, acted at every mile.
They plunder nursery; future's seedlings spindle.

Brutes rule these days.
Tinker the mind—
settlement mentality pays,
not character, culture for relevance.
We all retrogress rather than advance.
Worship of only money deserves protests.

Brutes rule these days,
highlight differences, grow mistrust in
society's strata saddled by strife.
Base instincts reign, raise green-thumbed farmers of
defalcation, malfeasance, debauchery, licentious thrusts,
primordial acts—a chest of horned hammers.

Brutes rule these days;
direct us to scatter, not gather
native wits for forays into
venues human deeds flatter.
In fake armour, they march on, unrepentant;
aroused common will, intolerant.

Brutes rule these days.
Celebrate, meditate!
Body so abused; mind slower frays.
Eat, drink, and dance, but never hesitate
to slip in your jigsaw piece—
extinction planes; brutes to no more rule any days.

DEEP DEFICIT

Guardians' fingers rifle soups
Sample field of bowls
Of embedded morsels in turns to all

Their hands crane to ensure
Largest morsels into their mouths
Other stomachs growl

Kindly tell me if you can
Is this how things are proposed
Surely there must be a name

Guardian angels work for free

DEFINE THE KINGPIN

What does it mean, to place in pride of place,
if general vibe is fittest survive?
From ultimate machine, select components debate;
sub-assemblies line up, supplicate.

The feet kick up dust and water, display their stock—
the sprint, the walk, the swim strokes, every mock.
"Out-of-danger, into pleasure, into activities . . .
we carry all there and back; we are the bosses."

"Recall, you all, a fence broadcasts your welcome.
Whatever the plan, whatever the goal,
if there's no action, there's nothing to show."
Hands self-indulge, clap for themselves.

Heart drumrolls quick beats—everyone shivers.
"If the beat goes on, I provide the beats.
I power food routes, symbolise life and love.
For these alone, I am the clear boss."

With no sweat, sweet duet, eyes perk ears,
"'It's a dangerous world' is a chorus so contagious;
off-their-rockers robots and more roam and maim.
We flag danger, show safe mangers, as bosses do."

"I am indeed the boss!" the brain—wall hangings shake.
"As general manager supreme, I control everything;
I tell everyone how and when to do things.
In senses sensible, what else makes the boss?"

After the no-mention act, anus shuts up, shuts down.
Toxics accumulate, circulate, debilitate—eyes puff up,
feet gain weight, hands dangle, heart hesitates.
Wet-soaked brain, elected envoy, mumbles apologies—

"It's a no-brainer; every role is part of the whole.
We all create waste, which must be flushed.
Kidneys-bladder-lungs-skin-nose routes do their parts too,
but no one, as we all *now know*, outdoes great ANUS.

We'll do all the work; Anus, you boss and pass out all the shit.
Need not be a brain to boss; just an asshole is now the fit."

AMBIGUITY

Souls to console, tales to restate
Egos to extol, quandaries to meditate—
Democracy Meritocracy Egalitarianism
Socialism Communism Capitalism
Antiquity Modernity Anarchy
One Society One Humanity.

Tips to mothers: optimise our parity;
tasks to parents: provide in quality.
Children drilled to believe—Life, even contest;
eat well, grow well, put in your best;
you'll take bows with no limit.
      Privileges play, foul plays commit.

Commanders recruit,
train, prime, promote pursuit.
Teachers illuminate charming possibility;
Peers impart resilient ductility;
employers mandate production for pay.
      Promise, equity, slipstream day on day.

Politicians convert human nature springboard—
"frame", "bait-and-switch" spill overboard;
our governance toast, theirs please roast;
we—the anointed! Paradigm shifts boast.
      Majority deprived, revenge revels;
      awake logic—there are no marvels.

Level field grows tracks otherwise fabricated.
Hate in creeps, abates; dark gorges elongated.
Afflicted, minds dull—warped perception.
Trickle-down prognostication turns deception.
>The now-life weighs in—gadgets, "moodies" remiss
>push more and more into more "in extremis."

Some researchers fart, their noses pinched;
directives galore, many quickly winched.
Security, others, put down—mothers undo.
Want then need then one-in-town, prized do.
>"Democraptalism" is capitalism's acquisition;
>"Commusocialitarism," operatives' ascension.

All governance facades aglow, same song sing—
"To all, the yields; only to few fling."
Rights turn handouts; majority scowl, howl,
in more ways than one, shout, "Foul!"
Double-talk glitches line up;
>tension, death, destruction hiccup.

Life with promise shared with equity;
floatable boats lifted—harbour, density.
Borderless world, fruit of the times.
Forge trends, shock grows with crimes.
>On wheels and tracks, a dreadful clash—
>food, supplies, many heads may bash.

Ancient lessons, new skills, chaos, weigh in, play!
Brightest beams—durable assay;
distribute same over Earth.
All life meaningful should berth.
>From the more provided, more is expected;
>paddle the waters, *YOU*, the lavishly curated.

FENCE OFF DECEIT

Millions of spermatozoa fly;
maybe, one shouts that cry.
A politics matrix
politicians fix.
If neighbour is one, raise fence high.

PROFILING

When profiling projects to defile, Bruiser Bear
only hibernating. Earth, the gift of gifts,
nurturing should caress. Particles-shield ruptures,
heat shields mature; seasons turn unseasonal,
cycles un-cycle; freezers thaw—rivers bloat seas;
wet-dry ratios rise, threaten—farmers fret, Small Island
Nations squirm; full model scrolls clutter carcases, waste;
post-assembly add-ons find reason—definite is not infinite.

When profiling projects to defile, Bruiser Bear
only hibernating. Nuggets persist, proclaim—
a beginning, a source, long ago. Species rear, spread;
towers, turrets, spires rise; moated fame, fortune
firm-up; stashers swell—rights, equity trodden;
golden crowns, lavish stones. Sky streaked,
the weak panic. The beginning, the source, in fake
darkness to hold future stores.

When profiling projects to defile, Bruiser Bear
only hibernating. Elder sits; his face, his stool in
age challenge: wrinkles versus cracks, wisdom versus time.
Hollow homage follows hollowed hallows—
falsehood images. Hints on deeds unheeded—
deeds so breaching, so foul; directions flawed;
heritage haemorrhaged frail, future in
demurrage; thinking deranged.

When profiling projects to defile, Bruiser Bear
only hibernating. That skin colour bears stories—

subcutaneous factories make vitamins;
rabbit breeding, group frivolity, attrition spiked;
lively lilts rage in riffs, howl.
Generations' sweat, tears, blood ignore;
goals score, sours goal or guillotine; backstory
vacate—dream up, act up, upend history.

When profiling projects to defile, Bruiser Bear
only hibernating. Holes a few are ordained,
one more for womenfolk. Structured anatomies,
perfect harmonies—roles designed, flows assigned;
no bruise nor fissure or lesion. Whims wing in,
impulses pulsate: proteins drilled into waste,
microbes; alkalis oppose acids.
Well-being wavers, vexes, verges.

When profiling projects to defile, Bruiser Bear
only hibernating. Alchemists in dubious
chemistries: more than pinches of toppers—
puffer-uppers; slow conveyor creaks,
scrapes, pauses. Caged, sardined birds
gorge; in weeks many collapse under own
weights; many "exit" to find peace;
more snide, ring up cash registers to please.

When profiling projects to defile, Bruiser Bear
only hibernating. Eye-catcher in fragrant wafts
drifts by—erogenous motion on Mars: curves
in proportions, face allure; necks strain, eyes trail,
breaths stay. Modelled-muscles struts by—
giggles, stolen snapshots, resolves. Stalkers
stalk, braggarts brag, strikes rack up.
Done gone, minds untethered but chipped, drift on.

SKIN COLOUR

Questions flood
Broken dykes spill crud
Ripostes recoil demure
Slacks beg for fillers
Squinted eyes roll away

Few stare facial muscles bunched
Restrained lips tremble
They scoot away from me
All about me but I must be
No mind rancour nor body odour

FORCED CHANGE

Ignorant racist needs bone marrow;
last chance donor, his colour horror.
"It's we do it quick, quick
or your life's last quirk."
"Let's go, Doc; my skin can turn that colour!"

PARITY DEBATE

"Equity, equality; what and how must they be?
Your five feet four, my six feet five don't compare;
I reach top shelf easy, you, three below viably.

My footprints—bold, my whereabouts declare;
you tiptoe on two sole points, detection faint,
claim your goings and comings are clear.

My voice booms, trespasser battles restraint;
your shaky, shrill voice—intruder thinks carrots.
Jimmied door creaks, you dash for cover, faint.

Left alone with the kids, they turn parrots—
on their butts, mimicking, manners afloat.
A whiff of me, they turn values, untold carats.

Our paycheques come in, a message to tote;
broken down to the hour, I'm in no playpen.
From notable difference, a statement to note.

Frail female soccer player wants same pay as for men,
though less entertaining and furthermore,
ratings dip. If they played naked, equal pay then.

I know, I know, you think me a pointless bore.
You're my wife, my partner, you must have a say;
make your points, your rejoinders, and more."

Pauses,   gears mesh, wheels spin—silent but play:
All these years, I raved freewheel; have I been fair?
The kids I speak out about, from start to today,

their journeys—she's chipped in more to their fare.
Our home would float, but for her as main anchor.
She's always wife, mother, counsellor with flair.

She's more—housekeeper, earner, without rancour.
Endurance unlimited, she calmly listened today.
I better hear her well; otherwise, I'm diabetic's sore!

"You know I fell for you on that first day—
roughs smoothen, lesions heal in time.
My knees callused; your remake I still pray.

Life and living, partnerships with rhyme
thrive most, the more equal every chime."

DOPPELGANGER

You slip into REM sleep; materialised wall
tall, massive—veils vast, dark vacuum.
Imagination sprouts mushrooms, oozes doses
that daze. Sounds fly past shunted ears.

Visual foxfire—surreal afar creatures,
uncountable spear-tipped tentacles.
What parts of the body will they pierce?
Leader glares; you stare back.

No, I must fight you freaks; I won't take nonsense!
You firm your stand ready to grab, pull, punch, or run.
You will your feet to test-tread fast; no motion—no
surface, no friction. More clearly you see them now.

Leader's mobile eyes emit five red targeting beams—
your eyes, your neck, your heart, your manhood.
Wet with sweat you power a scream—no sound.
Vile vermin, you mean to get me! Leader leaps nearer,

bares tusks for teeth, brown mucous sneer.
Where and why this encounter?
No answer. You shower in sweat;
down your spine streaks slide.

They wobble closer, chorus prefeast prayers.
Ugly freaks, you cannot have a god; why do you pray?
Leader lunges, tentacles seek five targets.
You coil up, spooked millipede; eyes clenched, palms crush ears.

You roar, expect multiple impacts—pain epicentres.
A figure, your doppelganger, interposes, glares down at you.
Grandpa's worn image; multi-coloured hair and beard, shaggy.
It's Grandpa all right; he was fond of me!

"You pitiful shrimp-wimp. You'll get another chance
if you repent. Lies upon lies to your devoted, lovely
wife disengages noble heritage. You hear!"
"Okay, okay, I'm so sorry; I won't do it again, I pro-o-mise!

Please Grandpa drive those freaks from me!"
"Freaks you call them? My platoon; they obey me
not a bit later than I bid—*NO MISS*. Now get, you imp!"
Pulls your ear: Taser! Taser! Taser! You bounce, vibrate,
energise shout, "Ah! I'm sorry!

Grandpa, I'm so sor————ry!" Your mumbles fade to sobs.
Tiny quakes, soft palm wipes your face, you wake;
creased forehead, searching eyes, puckered lips seek your face.
"Sweetheart. So much sweat, shakes, gabbles,   nightmare?"
"Nightmare can't compare . . . wraith scare or worse!

I must show remorse." You jump out of bed dash to shower.
Fresh sheets, PJs; you cuddle up, rehearsed to evade.
"Remorse? Sorry for what?"
"Sorry I woke you this late, love."
You ponder on a long while on—*How much
did she hear?*

THE ME

How dare I tell my indiscretions
My fib acquitted my friend Frank
I fibbed and know he's less than candid
Your judgement not too rigid

How dare I reveal my drivels
Tall tales you know I tell
Motorbike escape from park lions
No lions or motorbike during hike

How dare I air my secret passions
Paced-up group orgy with no apology
From urge to indulge I surf Internet
Delete history so you don't detect

How dare I declare my below-radar actions
My secret romp with Mary Jo
Your friend from the days of ties bow
Your friendship died more than slow

The many times lust devoured compassion
In my arms my secretary wailed her marriage bust
It got so hot we both lost mind
Iris forgot something worked in on us in the office

Instances my silence signalled wrong acquiescence
Violence-ridden neighbourhood cold slabs young men daily
I witnessed argument police arrive I walk
Murdered boy was innocent even peaceful

All those times of common sense distanced
Friends who stay out late I don't keep at bay
Lottery jackpot hunts thin my wallet
Sweets and sugars my dentist frowns then smiles

All those occasions deceitful
Piles of lies you smile at and don't delve
You fake blindness with so much finesse
My fickleness you best shelve

From emulsions oils float at last
Mints treat my mouth alcohol stench wells up
No more cigarettes my clothes tobacco smell
Calls and texts I delete escapees with tales foul

Clouds engulf caress welcome mountain peaks
Higher peaks that divert aviation
Create habitats in rarefied air versions
Seek to hide their protrusions

Surface-calm oceans deny commotion below
Predators and preys tussle play hide-and-seek
Man's intrusions spread scary waves alter chemistry
So much unseen so much mystery

From these blemishes I am leopard or cheetah
Each skin spot a stain from our vows I flout
Your gentle hand brushes off many a fault
Outer sheen seen of me you massage out

Still you urge me on in ways no one else can
How luckier can anyone be in clutter world
You are my armour my amour my ALTER EGO

For Rita Ann,
my dear wife.

THE PAUSE

I walk the beach with you,
snuggled; our feet stamp
limits of water reaches.

Our future bridges;
not frills or thrills,
but fits of twins.

Wet sand bears our feet,
stocks our words—sound bites
in cuddled footprints' bites.

Water rushes splash,
reflect sunlight—mobile beams
scan our fused frames.

White and blue water birds fly,
flutter white and blue flaps;
peace and love we agreed.

We can't walk the beach
until we die. We dress
to go, I look back—

Our footprints
are no more.
I exhale;

I . . .

FLOWER GARDEN PERFORMANCE

The serpent;
head held high,
a measure above ground,
fawns undeterred in pose.
Aromatic flowers' petals flutter.

The serpent;
tail dug in,
midsection coiled loose.
Body colours spruced up,
blend to blind.

The serpent
stays so still;
raised fore shears wind.
Dead leaves fly, fall;
pose is joist.

The serpent;
motionless glare.
Noise, movement ignored;
bride must be sight adored.
Patience pays.

The serpent;
such a vigil.
Could it be dance in a trance?
Meatiest bone links patient dog—
day-and-night vision vow.

The serpent;
nano-seconds' strike,
lightning full-length stretch.
Venomous fangs snap, discharge;
bride gripped by pangs.

The serpent;
all that show.
Great HOPES, but bitter blows—
poor lizard twirls in death dance,
no vows exchanged.

ROYAL BOY

Caught some tastes and made haste;
Tortured News labelled, "over roasted chicken."
"In a cosy evening," *Fair News* featured.
It's all been there for all to see, unmistaken—
Barroom, bedroom bedlam calls;
fakes from frames and fumes so false.

There's cause for pause;
long journeys' pauses pan and scan.
Africa's bowels erupt to disrupt—
"Little Foot" and "Lucy" set net of tethered,
not tattered, rungs of tongues sprung.
Streak a peek—the genome runs.

Alloyed stallion gambols regal;
stable facelift to noble stable.
Alloyed stallion deceit forfeits, runs
race of all races—royalty not penalty.
Alloys, gestalts, overtake components.
There's cause for pause to find pace.

Anthropology digs; reporter, DNA;
what, what . . . what a corralling say—
Rebellious rectitude, blood aptitude
propel nude attitude.

REDUCED ROLE

Monarchies some of the world rule;
king and queen, each a stool.
King is the crown,
queen not a clown.
Queen is crown; spouse, aide tool.

INSTANCES MOSAIC

Head down, brawny bull rushes,
spouts spew steam—stirred amblers
scamper, shout, push.
Bully bull careers . . .
Last fixed glare in abattoir.
¤   ¤   ¤
In the crosshairs, the choice—the crown;
trigger takes, town dismissed;
exodus scoped—MEMORY GORED;
invisible wound.

¤   ¤   ¤

Oestrus bitch barks, bluffs; sucks up in
thrust locked, the bleeding boss—
Prize fighter. Winner taker.
¤   ¤   ¤
Find old man in the dark—it's not hard.
A role failing to flow—weary blazer bled,
slowly fades.

¤   ¤   ¤
Death, death! To all at your pleasure.
Beats bend; tears streak, chin on feet;
silence for banter, chatter, laughter;
itches for caresses, warmth, spasms;
no-shows for bays, chairs, walkways.
Where's paraded resurrection?
Come mend—ASCENSION!

◻ ◻ ◻

Extreme lottery ticket ticks, fantasy moors—
feel-good wants, amnesia perverse.
Banker, taxman, seller, bilker, and more;
predators all, posture, wish to reverse—
tank-up, hanker . . . New robes, new car,
new will; new taste buds, new life.
Sobering exposés!

◻ ◻ ◻

From rat race into Premier League chase,
backwoods team chests trophy; owners, coaches,
players, fans, reporters in group orgy.

◻ ◻ ◻

Frightened, hungry migrant in rickety contraption;
escapade rations of foamy tosses, sharks,
deep dark blue. Improved life HOPE
felled by blade.

◻ ◻ ◻

Indigenes in deeds with nature;
nuns, monks in monasteries;
all they now miss, are they in bliss
now or in the future?

◻ ◻ ◻

Years of slanderous inquisitions end—
in small soft wrap, new joy alive
slumbers; new start, new
status, new plans.

¤   ¤   ¤

When instances settle, sort, sum up, sell lure,
and past looks through present to future true,
banners and brass bands, out quick, please do.
Expressive boogies too!

BEGGING HARMONY

Patrimony gifted flashes marriage proposals, buys frayed nerves,
sleeps alone—losses losers log. Court with caution;
shun half-done vision
in rapid motion.

◻ ◻ ◻

History settles, memory melds; campaigns political globally trend:
cash
moves, words in wards—targets flummoxed. Number hordes,
sleight-of-hand. Voters vote, what's been gained?
Same old issues once more vexed.

◻ ◻ ◻

Court adjourns without a plea; plain takeaway—
accused woman spends days to next session
quartered with rape suspects
in court's guesthouse.

◻ ◻ ◻

Engineer screams, expletives explode, "A lateral fin for a vertical fin;
cords dangle, legging crooked, weight overbears.
Heliport out of sort; the plans are clear!"
Privileged, but plans-blind builder.

◻ ◻ ◻

Belief in self, belief in others; fast-bond agents, symphony of HOPE
regales fulfilment. Accord, accord, sullied on the sword—
wide rifts, rancour cuffs;
friendship dies.

◻ ◻ ◻

Comedy and tragedy, opposed entertainment—ribs ache, tears dry.
Good bets; encores endorse when experts engage. Tension;
greenhorns play—patrons change theatres,

furious for refunds.

◻ ◻ ◻

Board members spin profit tales; detailed tailored, every facet.
Loudest to media eager for up-takes; the piped to workers
via management; golf course tips on political donations;
hefty theirs—fancied furtive footers.

◻ ◻ ◻

Hold on please—bits, pieces, threads,
different wards; I can't locate
an epiphany!

Ah jagged chords of Begging Harmony.

FENTANYL "FIXES"

Streets, all turned battlefronts;
hawk-eyed "Narcos" do hunts.
Suspect and evidence
they haul within fence.
Boss checks both for charge counts.
Public Park is across, a stone toss.
There they troupe—suspect, "Narcos," Boss.
They strip naked,
dance so wicked.
"Who will halt lusty shows?" viewers fuss.

MONEY HILLOCK

Anti-anxiety pharmaceutical magic—
Anxiolytic, psychedelic, hypnotic.
Mesolimbic reward pathways tick;
Money hillocks grow prolific.

Robust pipelines, robust defence lines;
strong shareholders, strong interest.
Commanders, foot soldiers all frontline—
dangled measly imprest.

Business schools bestow strong trails—
Expand: forward-, backward-integration;
maximise fast, optimise as profit entails.
Multilateral actions in risk alleviation.

PROMOTIONS

Uppers, downers, all-arounders' promotion—
COMMOTION! Accommodation for emotions.
Intentions intuitive huddle outsized options;
native glands, native hormones, net neglect.

Hesitant, yes, toddler learns gravity, balance;
off floor, toddler explores more and more.
So many cheer; so many more tear. Dalliance—
animated toddler beams, "Lots more to floor!

Bassinette, pram, cot, playpen too often cramp;
I aim to choose, I aim to move, camp to camp."
Wobbly steps to escape wet stinking diapers;
much more to wrestle—allure, grabbers.

Toddler turns sprinter supreme; races, hazes.
Many coaches preach many approaches.
Sprinter—spire on fire—blazes, sucks, puffs.
Sprinter runs, hazes; runs, hazes.

Sprinter is spire on fire; blazes, sucks, puffs.
Runs, blazes, hazes; runs, blazes; runs . . .

LYNCHED

Signal tower of moral rectitude;
disdain tower to corniness;
robust crane that lifts attitude.

Stripes you clip on from firmness
at school, in family.
Your work spheres, sturdiness.

You run schedules calmly;
you both dote on only daughter;
people relate rather fondly.

Life's on zephyrs—minimal clutter.
You both wonder how long
the run before a halter.

Memoir narratives' song—
"Choir of packed events,
light and darkness jointly sung.

Circumstance circumvents
cherished trends, dreams,
without prior comments.

How exact the scope beams?
Paradigms shift, fake carrots galore;
fouled dice throw, it often seems.

Game plans unreviewed, conjure
muddled backyards, evince
yens—sermons' results offshore."

Fate's cruel; hits without a wince.
Job loss, house loss, flag on
hailstones that echo,   still bounce.

Wife, daughter on fateful dawn,
lost in fatal crash—
DUI driver; wrong lane, fast run.

Total solar eclipse—a rash flash.
No face or voice cushions shock;
fast drawdowns on your IOU stash.

Weeks on, still rundown luck.
Father off hospice, stiff and cold;
mother-in-law enters hospice block.

School dropout friend takes hold.
Family, friends, bow out;
moods that smother, hurtful, unfold.

Rehab-relapse rotor cycles, no doubt—
arms, legs, hips, strangely tattooed;
general debility, pinpoint pupils, shout.

You're not alone—many more pooled;
twists and turns, rooted callous greed.
Whole wide world trapped, schooled.

If the UN is common-voice agreed,
life so REWIRED is gang-murder decreed.

MIRROR IMAGES

commotion
imprecision
immolation.

shoot-out
shoot-from-the-hip
shoot-up.

CHUCKLES

See every woman as your loving mother.
Don't ever forget; you'll forever be buoyed.
"Oh yes, I quite agree, but my father—
ravenous, eventually self-destructed."

◻ ◻ ◻

View everyone, not impending bother;
sooner surely, you'll harvest no tears.
Chilled, draped, sidewalk sleeper beggar,
"Quiet zone please; drop only notes, CHEERS!"

◻ ◻ ◻

American tourist—boisterous, I CAN spirit.
Into night, Rosie regales Jideh: ideas, events,
people all big, special home-state-Texas ways.
Breakfasting, Jideh, "True Texan, you . . . capacious."

◻ ◻ ◻

Bonered, fostered young stud must offload.
Pre-paid hooker voluptuous, skilfully unravels,
booty bares. Young stud glares, brims, shivers,
"Ah ah ah, wo-o-oh!" Hooker rekits, "Job done!"

◻ ◻ ◻

A week tonight, it was "BEAUTIFUL!" you hollered for
BATTERY FULL. Tonight it's "TURN HER ON!" for TIMER ON.
Beloved husband, if my phone you must spy on,
use your eyeglasses for *goodness* sake!

◻ ◻ ◻

Direct, unflinching to experience, to know;
up-and-about Vickie, so on-the-go.
All makes, all shapes guys, gals pounce and go.
Vickie's granny, "Save something for your hubby!"

47

□ □ □

Mysterious humankind, loaded richer with age—
hair, silver blazes; dentition, bold gold; kidneys,
precious stones; high-grade sugar in blood; gas pockets;
choice metals in joints; prized world stage.

□ □ □

Erratic husband to wife, "For you, I will go
to the end of the cosmos—the brightest jewels!"
Wife retorts, "You watch too many promos; I hope
your gyros fails—ah those ceaseless duels . . ."

□ □ □

Chancy Charlie fancies Dean's List.
Every evening, his coin toss, "Heads, it's Laurie
I'll see; tails, movies and sleep;
stand on edge, I study hard all night."

□ □ □

Troubled ugly hubby to wife, "My modelled manly
body or my fine face, which one gets you most?"
Calm wife replies, "I'd be damned by a wild boast.
Let's see now . . . your sense of humour, it is!"

□ □ □

Fraternal twins buzz hospital loud, long;
some relations wonder too. In every detail, twins are
different, DNA later had a say. Frowning father fumes,
"Share, lockstep, with my best friend?"

□ □ □

Still unsure Toby to Tina, "How many boyfriends
before me?" Long silence without pretence prompts
Toby, "Why the silence?"
"I'm still counting."
"Wao-o-oh, I'll be lost in there, the count that is!"

□ □ □

Chafed, choked Susie seeks small lift—new SIM card,
sexiest voice, calls hubby in dining, "H-e-l-l-o dar-ling!"
Husband, "Call you later love; monster's in the kitchen."
Emergency, emergency: off-the-fire-soup-on-a-face!

◻ ◻ ◻

Hunky migrant, baptised imminent immigrant,
struggles, flirts out apprentice grocery-driver job.
"Your starting salary is 4,500."
"Thanks much ma'am. Please ma'am,
what's the riding salary?"

◻ ◻ ◻

First-time tension suffuses; family friend, Billy, is around.
Waters broke. "My car behind yours; use my new horn!"
She whispers to husband. Rush-hour traffic, street carnival—no trouble.
Rapid gunshot sounds over wailing sirens—the new horn.
Oh-oh   Chorusing squad car fleet floods ER!

GUTTED AFRIKA GUSHES

From my womb from my wounds
    ID codes embedded—backstory permanent. Herd on range—
    lead members, shepherds. Elongated umbilicals to first suckling.
    Group victories from behaviours proper—inspiration.
    Liberator of self, multitude others, be;
    CREATOR who rules SUPREME, I am not.
    Me,   at the start with dreams for future.

From my womb from my wounds
    Daring vanguard, upkeep platoons
    ripple, settle,   calluses.   Permanent rearguard—
    my far-off gerontology care.   Rise, migrate, propagate.
    Cajole leases, blend with hosts. Fear not, share inventions.
    My aura overarches,   inundates.

From my womb from my wounds
    Subtleties abound in lives lower: cuddles,
    wobbles, wriggles, backbones, fracas; cycles in
    regenerative scenes . . .   The mantis prays, the mantis preys;
    some felines, fox-like; camel drinks—long spell;
    bear hibernates well; wasp preys bee, bee showcases
    hierarchy, order, teamwork.

From my womb from my wounds
    Chameleon be if you must—survival dyes. Rabbit,
    panda, phylum annelid, all bear assays; many more!
    Rhythm for rhyme, music, dance, entertainment, all morph in
    reserves—off-times' chimes proffered.
    Enzymes and genius fires on soles, wheels, floaters, wings.
    Mellowed doctrinaire segues for mind, for body.

From my womb from my wounds
Behold!   Mutinies in family, often instigated.   Phobia
everywhere seek prefixes—XENO prized, more breathe down.
Genocide homicide, placebos for fratricide
monstrous,   huge;
forced shoulders to wheels, forced hands to crafts—mean, demeaning.
Miscegenation on whim—shadows foul. My forced
abortions: gaseous,
liquid, solid afterbirths carted away.
My wounds my vacuums . . .

From my womb from my wounds
Here, there, and about, owners turned squatters secluded;
taunted, excluded in ways awful from yields.
Wanton milieu muggings, reckless.
Greed-enthroned envy flares, death glares.
"Extremers" ice bound see   sunrise sunset   inch on from
long-set beacon sets. Princely Traveller's Palm echoes.

From my womb from my bowels
Links to foundation quakes. Taller, taller mountain waves crash,
crush, poach in folds. Ambiguity reigns—roots plough deeper;
leaves pastel; rivers bloat, slim.   Gravity centre shifts—
gravity moments;
orbit cryogenic or orbit that sinters.   Tempers foolish—
triggers: BOOM-BOOM!
maxi-mini novas! Meteors, meteorites flash away; asteroids'
orbits unknown;
water sheets, balls, orbit their ways.

From my womb from my bowels
Reciprocity, retribution, reparation, equity all play and stay only
tests of flimsy membranes.   Strained, drained, denied,

51

I've been cast off—outboard, outpost for supplies. Dumpsite—
the damaged damagers.

ELEVATED MULTIPLE CARRIAGEWAYS LOOM TO BOON!

Come home, come home to a retreat—
hold hands, sing, skip, dance;
striped festival for all; a festival of victory over dark
chasms, vision blocked by false rays.
The family reunion FRATERNAL on my invite—no delays.
Evoke me!

How many more wrong rows . . .?
Come home! Come home! Come home!
Come home HOPE macro . . .
My "darkness" fails to stop
piss-backs, heists' outflows
from my womb from my bowels from my wounds.

HARMATTAN

Sahara Desert blows dust,
early November to mid-March,
envelops West Africa.
Ferocious, December-January.

Mother continent—large, diverse;
winds howl, doors creak, roofing sheets clap;
apparels flail unless starched;
trees sway, tunnel sights to vistas grey.
Windows whistle alerts.

Forgotten masses trudge on—food must be tabled.
As in equatorial ovens or winter freezes,
more grit, more eye wipes, more sneezes.
Life must go on, they can't afford to hoard;
they feel lucky in minimum room and board.

The skin is ashy, needs oil.
Afflictions roar, angle spoils.
Temperatures dip—evaporative cooling;
folks bundle up, goats bleat.
Forget housekeeping, nothing is neat—
dust, dust, dust!

Pilots' vision obscured, planes stay put;
only heard are planes that dare.
Cotton blinds loaded;
as filters, improve room air.
Subterfuge may arise; no joke!

Pathogens, toxics, set on rides—
fumigate, force region contagion.
Muck from afar,
dispersers inserted, volatilise raindrops.
The region will fret damn all fits.

Harmattan, Harmattan,
you must have some fine shine.

"Ah yes, I do: I cool everything down;
global warming gets tiny brakes.
I stabilise soils, foliate feed plants.
I warp woodwork to rate joinery takes.
I reduce confrontations; there are fewer rants.
I task skimpy dressers; fewer fogeys frown.
I power wind turbines.
I suck, puff on lit cigarettes, conserve health.
I force embraces for more love to bless."

For AMAKA WELUGEWE ANINGO,
my granddaughter,
born during Harmattan.

EXPECTATIONS

Weary warriors, worn out from battle,
high sea ledge downplays ocean waves,
huddle, recline, refresh; action heroics prattle.

Vantage point—safety and beauty raves.
Distant views surround; thank goodness—
apparition tales; all what their god craves.

Countless comrades killed: goodwill, openness.
"Let whoever, whatever come, our peace
overcomes—water off granite hardness."

Granite pieced though, loses molecular lease.
Much con and bile, so vile, welcome shatters,
then blinds soul's eyes to deep greed disease.

Horizon specks where blue water, sky matters
edge. More visible, intriguing; time marginal.
Features form: images on floaters—squatters?

Warriors cluster, ponder sight so subliminal;
many anchors for brave action sagas seed.
Lost in wonder, some spew sayings nominal.

Duty call—warriors stand guard, as need.
Yelling, few rush home, "Sight unfolds fast;
defence ensemble to shoreline with speed!"

Three floaters with cargoes, more loaded the last,
slowly drift in, five hundred metres from shore
they stop; strident warriors' horns, drums blast.

People, warrior numbers, on shore to ensure
ridge of will and fight heighten, any evil repel.
Senior elders alerts—insights aboard reassure.

Two, three days' standoff, a move must compel
measures safe: Elders return home, contemplate.
Hours' debates: fear or fight they vow to dispel.

Elders return to shore—huge moot court template!
Shoreline half mile: people, warriors; horns, drums—
warning beats day and night shake Earth's under-plate.

Diplomacy dulled; far removed from recalled proms,
setting tasks elders. Some jumpy nerves they becalm,
"King's hours away; his strong aversion to maelstroms.

His orders—clear, predictable, not a single qualm—
You say they look like humans; oceans don't grow forests.
They'll cherish our kindness; not a clenched palm.

Three brave swimmer-warriors paddle to GUESTS;
lead them to berth; wash off awful white dye.
The hell they must have seen, only in felons' chests.

Under dye, see and trust, they are like us. Try!"

OYOFO OGHE COMMUNITY

Disunity raids community, vicious pickpocket.
Opportunities propitious explode to implode;
directions contrary—fictitious, malicious.
Immunity lost; everyone on docket.

Opportunities propitious explode to implode
from ego overload—capricious, less wisdom.
Immunity lost; everyone on docket.
No whammy or magic so tragic.

As egos overload, capricious to shared wisdom,
community ego mutates to ethos, then eros.
No magic or whammy so tragic.
Rescuer—common spirit's forceful tick.

As community ego mutates from ethos to eros,
reality should dawn—common destiny trips up.
Rescuer, communal spirit's loudest tick—
every view, common review, no previews.

Reality dawns—shared destiny trip-ups.
History, heritage, times must zip-up
all views, common review, no previews because
disunity raids community as vicious pickpocket.

> For Oyofo Oghe, my community,
> now in change-induced retreat from
> Afrikanness.

POSITIVE CHANGE

Some are born with much promise for sure
Make community glues bond to endure
Seal fissures fractures
Oyofo Ngamikpo rebounds
Flashes radiant splendour
Veritable heritage restaged managers
Agents of Positive Change
Through "Ezi elo n'igbambo" mission
(Proactive ideas and action mission)
Noble Ancestor Spirits' waves market vision
Not man-made but all HIS PLEASURE

For my mentees,
UCA Age Grade
of Oyofo Oghe

SERVICE CALL

Stoic in battle with swamp mosquitoes, my son calls,
"Daddy, no sleep, pricks! Huge hypodermics
thud my PJs! The pain! The itch!
If I crush one, crimson stains. Will it be malaria or
filaria for me?"

I imagine choppers whirl dissonant, bounce on
dilapidated helipads—a script from these times.

"Okay, son," I say, "after camp, you'll be posted;
hosts' ripostes aplenty.
Overcome, do more.
Immure downers, embrace thrills.
National Youth Service endows stature. Recall,
son, your siblings hail, 'Compatriot!'"

A script from these days or trans-generational
fractures of ages sprinkled with patriots?

Compatriots of patriots; three main traits.
Total picture undistracted by miniature—
lake's water level sums tributaries' inflows.
Assess the obverse, the reverse—
justice offsets prosecution, defence pleas.
Patriots scale hurdles, face friable overhangs;
hoist flag atop mountain!

Scripts enliven the days; scripts enliven the future;
Scripts leaven backstory; scripts cast all in picture.

About the mosquitoes, I say, "Move into a wing with
more people, son; ratios may crumble, tumble, decay."

For my son, Chidume, at the NYSC assignment,
a compulsory post-graduate government programme
that alleviates Nigerian tribalism
by exchanging youth to volunteer
in respectively unfamiliar communities.

ELECTRIFIED IGBO NATION

Take a view, a good full view—
panoramic, dynamic.
Greatness titles spew,
every sentence from every view.
Deserted, common sense—
solo sails perilous demote cruise.

Bursting country in darkness
seeks light and forgiveness.
Operators are assigned—
generation-transmission-distribution.
Who gets what bunch, for how much?
Agendas launch.

Igbos lock in lucky freedom actions;
generation-transmission-distribution.
Freedom colour dons callous pallor—
gash deeper, deepen darkness,
chase bank credits so obsessive;
Igbos in demerits so invasive.

They leave "work posts," flock "mountain fires,"
pretend to inspire spires higher.
Maggots don't build flesh;
termites terminate wood deck strength;
erosion washouts bite tyres.
Pause to construe a true course—

Creed-decreed community communes
atop plateau that cranes necks.
Sacred segues assured—
Splendid soldier-guardians on chariots of time
clamp down crime, vaporise rime.

The shine—So Sane   So Tame   So Sublime . . .

PUNGENT COMMODITY

Woman steady seller in pepper market
chokes, sneezes, swaggers, hollers;
logic lost, ambience lofted.

Eyes-nose-face, no touch;
down below   oh-oh   a no-no!
Buyers she frisks; money into pouch.

Repeat buyers count not much—
hurried smiles, hurried hellos;
primary prey, queasy sneezer.

Heat and tang raise fumes.
Long-term engagement grows fangs,
sharper tusks in the ill-bred seller.

Holed-up seller, deprived long, dreams
liberty launches in extreme—
money to splash, escape from pen.

Sweat drops streak, she jeers
with drops of tears, no fear.
Heartbeat thumps, seeks calmer days.

Wired wily seller lures, shifts;
pendulum swings—green then red.
Inner torment, fulcrum, stays steady.

Pepper seller amalgam, IED terrible—
pocket-stripper, strip-teaser, multi-feelers
poison-tipped, chameleonic octopus.

Pepper market woman seller wrangles,
angles selfish angles.

OBLIVION

Mobile corpse gambles
Blind to when how the end
Mobile corpse no-mend timed
Tick-tock or with chimes
or glides in perfect stealth

Spend not effort to watch clock
Dutifully do as it always does
Move count amble sides
A fair cop to bouncy bud or fogey
This for sure rebuts hokey

From the terrace of sinkholes
The common playground
The elephant disappears   The ant disappears
The sinkhole-littered promenade
Springs forth Phallic Mound

Mobile corpse no-mend timed
Blind to when how the end

THE FADE

ZIP ZAP ZING   YEAH
Energy flurries pour
Oh the games you now play
Your tactics tracks lay bare
Memory's shine in decline

Moments stories erstwhile notable
Creep in fade out disjointed
Many threads inscrutable
No matter how earlier remarkable

Toxins mature proxy free
Microbes pathogens easily spree
Mind far outraces body
Immunisers shadow lazy shoddy

Skin thinned springs
Lungs harden fight to belong
Tardy liver tarries
Kidneys in Disneyland distracted

Setting sun displays
Garnered wise rays

PASSAGE PERMIT

Chisels, chiselling chisels . . .
Nature, society,
parents, siblings, community;
you, me!
You want to be; I want to be.

Need, want, dream, aspiration,
expectation, imposition all fly sly—
directions, confrontations, explosions,
flashes, death all fly high;
orphans cry, parents sigh.

Widows wallow, exacting swallow;
associates cringe, comrades binge.
Logic shallows, reasoning unhinge.
You take this and I take that,
for peace and progress, falls flat.

Resources moan, the planet groans;
supplies use abuse.
Boggling, harsh light years for loans?
Mock immediacy, court a ruse;
corral the planet, loosen the noose.

All the hurry to shutter, to body bag.
Surely, eventual end—
yesterday him; today her.
Bits of time, bits of opportunity,
for all more often should billet and fend.

Science and technology can open doors—
rich pastures, not oppressive moors.
Oneness, evenness;
spikes of "haves" often rupture
beauty and love in our nature.

You there, me here; no picket line.
You to be, me to be; fine.
Extreme passion or intense compassion?
Latter, please, for journeys of fashion;
journeys on more than passage tickets.

GOLDEN GATES

History houses mysteries as hot spots on.
Lasting perception has to be won;
thread story first, debates can rage.
Minds events, imbue hue, in support—
whinging truth will whine out no report.

Paper, pen, keyboard, and screen providers;
storyteller and listeners;
jailer and prisoners;
rapist and the raped;
the phobic and the pariah;
the looter and the looted;
the exalted and the halted;
the vociferous and the voiceless;
the executed and the executioners;
all the rest of us, in the cast.

Short-term pay you pray;
long-term, we all pay.

Eternal story remains—
truth lives timeless;
we all swam same currents;
same "cosmics" shower us all;
we all drank from same fountain;
we all come naked then go portfolio-less;
medical science ceaselessly choreographs alliance.

TRUTH

I'm defaced, still I prosper;

I better, I glitter,

I evoke desire.

Comments, torments flatter;

I liberate.

Gigolo is true litter,

prostitute's fame, lame.

Roles I don't claim.

Nomad without title deed;

I hibernate,

I reincarnate,

I invigilate.

Breeder reactor, my streaming teems,

defines HOPE.

NEVER TOO LATE

"You can't teach no old dog no new tricks!"
Cliché colloquial that says more, undone.
"You don't learn left-handedness in old age!"
Forerunner African adage of ages pre-sages.

Orthopaedics wing hashes heart, mines mind—
limbs wrecked limp or stiff, dangle or swing;
frames reframed, braced to re-circuit marrow;
stripped flesh, shattered bones, to mend.

Crafty hands, painkillers, pick HOPE to rebuild.
You visit to bring cheer, but lumps you gulp,
wonder who makes the decisions and how.
Sweets and sours, mutually exclusive, unfair.

Diced fresh tuber, spliced, sprouts jollity lifts;
roots sink and spread, leaves fan out and fan.
Entire wing echoes Credo's return from yonder;
he came in lumps, each lump crushed but cope.

Short nights lead long days in first weeks;
bones, flesh, skin, sinews, veins, grafts, all auto-suture.
His whale of a will wills and commands the actions;
wing asphyxiates with passions of celebrations.

Credo's monikers come faster than weeks creep by—
Chairman, Storyteller, Comedian, Lover Boy . . .
small sample from caregivers' and co-patients' takes.
Credo grows into wing's fountain of mirth and fun.

Female caregivers bend over him, a hand over
chest; male caregivers come, bull-faced, ready for
cluster-bomb snipes; donors take note, tower the
fountain—his special wheelchair climbs steps.

Eagerly, he bears demands, no one else
dares, upstairs to director's office that
succumbs. Your lucky visit falls on Credo's
discharge day. Wing is leaked balloon, flabby.

Animated Credo, non-stop performer, bounces in
rhythm with his words. Wheelchairs and passengers,
caregivers and visitors crowd discharge lobby.
Quips and snipes—laughter and applause.

Credo pauses, scans faces;   lungs refill, he
struggles with discharge papers.
"My left hand did it," he shouts, "It did it.   See!"
Waves his filled forms and pen with his left hand.

His stubbed knees and right elbow point in possible directions.
His wheelchair climbs van ramp, he bellows,
"Priced right,   CHANGE,   never too late;   HOPE is key.
Melissa the kisser; my love letter soon, you sexy mate."

BOOT CAMP

It makes sense to believe world is of teams;
everything alive schooled, part of a team.
Special school for Peacock, Billy Goat, Tony,
Julie, Tom, Kekovsung, Hatcher, species' reps.

Grey display on, wind-swayed Peacock trots upfront;
prized peahens only mate to enhance species' traits.
Thick-skulled Billy Goat butts its way to kids' feed bin;
general feed bin holds fodder enough for days.

Tony's answers turn teacher's face frontline;
smile and scowl vie to control her facial muscles.
Bright Tony, his antics frost the air stinky thick.
Mirror-under-teacher's-table ploy pulled his school seat.

Accountant Tom, auditor Julie manage cash spigots.
Well-documented, acclaimed; they have big offices.
Overhead tank fills up; every point—flow, lullaby.
Unseen furloughs puzzle; leaks empty overhead tank.

Kekovsung, his power team, front privatisation—economy cure;
efficiency, capitalism's by-product, saves the day.
Self-letting, rent-seeking foray, promote decay;
they erect their quota of high prison watchtowers.

Bias—basic in nature's life nests, special in humans;
extreme in people, dignity ruptures.
Hatcher's fortress sits in Freedom Neighbourhood;
years on, no neighbour sees the inside.

That special school staff with daring prefects,
re-think, re-educate—powers of friendship.
Every life finds HOPE—future with promise;
Earth's waves wave to Universe that echoes.

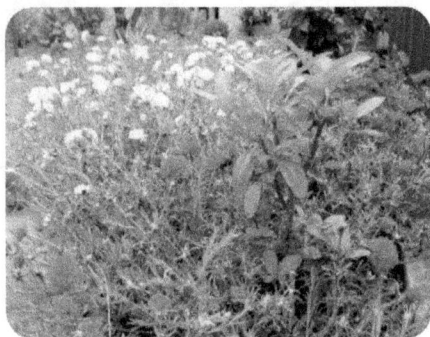

Madiba

endowed but bowed

furious over-reaches to bridge

burns heartstrings well-done

epic burden for apex guerdon

foes' faces minds woebegone

eternal enabler soars

noble human spirit roars

preaches food on rotary conveyor

equitable blind selections

all as if on revolving doors

inheritors correctly tend tours

ah dalibhunga, founder of council

ah madiba, revered clan icon

FATHER

Neither a paladin nor a tub thumper
do I intend to be for our dear father.
But as far back as memory carries me,
no one walks the Earth as he.

In furthest recesses, he still looms.
The boom falls hard on scanty occasions;
his cheer clears tears on more rotations.
No stomach growls—his trowels bring.

Bricks and mortar erect wall of life.
Winds may whistle, sun may singe,
rains may soak, but the wall still stands.
That's what he says of wall of life.

Plaster and paint, he warns, emit images—
backdrops for photos, markers to see,
activities within, shield against intruders . . .
Nothing stands without bricks and mortar.

Each brick comes compact, baked.
Different bricks line up, form a course;
bricks for straight runs, bricks for corners,
special bricks for special effects.

Courses rise one on the other until height.
Most vital, he says, is function-might of mortar—
decisive agent, carries and holds bricks;
agent he humanises, as he wears others' skins.

Over time, he gives life to each brick type.
Emotions ready to explode he caresses calm;
spaces that crowd he grows with chamfers.
His methods, parables, cheer make him agreeable.

When minds don't meet in community meetings,
brickbats in acrobatics fly—volcano spits rubble.
Bricks fall—jumbled heaps.
Corona of his aura peeps; bricks line up, form a course.

His great-grandchildren swim in public lake,
dip their noses in ripples his splashes create.
Best of all is whenever a wall blocks me,
he still counsels on escape manoeuvres.

Surreal maybe, but so real to me.
He frontloads instructions to guide generations.
The Puppeteer General marches on, thunders.
Forewords to why no one walks the Earth as he.

EVERYONE'S MAMA

Number of years reviewed,
it feels like a sprint—
Usain Bolt in glory.
Packed memory unpacked,
another story—
Prized diamond glitters;
every side reflects light,
colourless purity,
every quality hardy . . .
"Gem" is a weak word.

Only days ago, it seems.
Breastfeeding warmth;
body heat, climate control;
detective's eyes, nonstop duty—
every itch gently scratched,
every grunt well researched,
pinpricks denied sticky ticks.
Meet-the-world routines
choreographed in details,
in plots of many sequels.

Only days after, it seems.
Sequels swirled, swept in
three war-prone warriors,
two gender images revelled—
every scrape quickly salved,
intellect fed on nutritious diet.
Consanguinity unlimited,
whole community on tow—
kitchen churned, hunger hanged;

waterhole belched, thirst fled;
arrow on bow returned to quiver.

Only days after, it seems.
Troves of behaviours as must-tow—
each action in sensible nuance;
when you must, pounce.
Mariner is winner who reaps
zeal from each sea toss.
Love drenches hate trenches.
Accuser be, if you must, not the accused.
Stretches in others' skins, clues
empower. Dinners shared endear
digestion. Helping hand, a ladder rung.
Group matches reap power.
Lunch pack is personal; festival, public.

Only days after, it seems;
104 years are 104 days,
wisdom rains still shower.
Amazed by examples, community still
shouts, "One of a kind—mind,
soul, MAMA AFRIKA!"   Your sobriquet
branders stole to market rice.
Oh money-minded missteps.
Flashback bubbles, flashback humbles,
best against trouble.

Sun shines sunnier; night promotes vision.
MAMA AFRIKA, thanks for the
privilege. Your voice,
still strong—we shun wrong,
load up HOPE.

MASTERSTROKE

Pursuant to leavened targets on
People doing what's to be done
Believe they do their love to do
Leader's masterpiece
Epic stroke that lustre gains
From servant-leader mien retained
Positive production promoted

BUDGET AIR TRAVEL

Redemption isn't exemption, diced and spliced anyhow.
Barebones budget airline tickets eked out all year long—
all wallets on hunger strike; family adopts vacation bow.

Busted breakfast, wee hours flight, bathroom unsung.
Surprise confirmation—airport buzzes, we're not alone.
Sun still hidden, asleep; fakers fake whatever, belong.

Not all are decked out; many dress light, parry loans.
All on my own, I fancy action, most options' fits—
jeans, varied tops; I pledge laughter outshouts groans.

Adolescent pranks I tie to bedpost, but reputation bits!
Oh well, I enjoy chocolate bars with nuts, now and then.
Mummy, sister Julie, radiate pleasure—catchy hits.

Lo   behold, neighbourhood family, house number ten;
snide snipes—race, class, religion, country, world beats.
You talk weather, sports, "I'm late!" you restrain.

They wave heartily, stop by us—no vacant seats.
We watch; they scatter into crowded departure gate space.
Each one bubbles, babbles—topics hardly earn repeats.

Airline, passengers, well acquainted, every action says—
one hour, thirty minutes delays twitch not a facial muscle.
Cheap holiday travel mood—patience, savvy, slow pace.

Banter, chatter everywhere; BOARDING sign earns no hustle.
I observe, I muse a while—*to heed chitchat is to be polite.*
My carry-on I nestle, muscles strong, not much to rustle.

Row of ten, two window seats, Daddy flags me window right;
Mummy Julie Daddy, on my left, two seats and an aisle away.
It's still dark outside, but low energy bulbs shower light.

Tiny vibrations, masked engines' hums—"hello" takes sway;
overhead bins loaded, we learn our space until daytime.
I think ten thousand metres up and night changes to day.

I peek—view sprawls; blurred figures, lights sublime;
green, amber, red, clear, blue pattern out; service trucks roam.
I imagine what and how many bits-and-pieces for flight-on-time.

Interior décor comfy, only essentials adorn our five-hour home.
Seat belt signs, announcements, gentle tug—airplane creeps,
slowly speeds up, speedy pace to tarmac stand—blinks on dome.

We get flag-off; engines roar, torque up, anxiety leaps.
Hush dense; some eyes close perhaps prayers; backrests busy.
Two hundred plus focus—pilots' good luck must be in heaps.

Off start blocks, inners sink, seats pay dues; first-timers dizzy.
Seconds of top sprint on tarmac, tension halos, holds, until lift-off;
so imperceptible, so smooth a glide up—complexity looks easy.

Tension depletes, whispers grow louder at steady level off;
cautious movements; merchandise trolleys crawl aisles.
Everything's for sale; *smiles and seatback adjustment payoff?*

I peer out again, all ablaze metropolis fans out miles and miles.
I ponder: *all this energy, engine thrusts, passenger telepathy;*
do they combine to avail lift-off tension demise, relief in smiles?

At dawn we land; *the forces again combined? Inverse duty?*
Off airport—days of sights, events, food, drinks, all "on the tee."
"Danny take this, Danny take that," I get everyone's empathy.

Exotic cuisines that can't find me later, but I swear to better me.
Forget fringe frills; it's magical—days with no frown on a brow!
Barebones budget airline tickets, for so many, so very dreamy.

Redemption isn't exemption, whether diced and spliced anyhow;
recreation from stress, work, or weather deserves some kowtow.

TAKE A CHANCE

Skin-and-bones boy often walks by at dinnertime.
The soles of his shoes give his frame lifts in beats;
his trousers' legs crease, as if they sit on his shoes;
a shirt on a bedside hanger images his top on him.

You and your household often talk about him.
None of you has spoken to or know him by name;
threats of the times—much fear, much frost.
To be fair, though, he looks calm, clean, and neat.

Plunge,   invite him in for some food and drinks.
Guess,   sit him down by your kids his peer.
They ease him in—intros to banter;
diplomat's garb on, get to know him.

Everyone is a library; each book, bestseller.
Tweak stories—how truly one we all are!
Nothing so far said breaks the bank or the law.
It's possible he's later your prized son-in-law.

WICKED INVITE

Take a break, your desk will rest;
few birds fly Cape Town-New York.
Come to me; come with me and play.
Stay today—other days, other plays.

Beaver pauses to mate;
wrecking balls not on duty 24/7;
dynamite puck in pipe vanishes in explosion;
elephant in flight,   rainbow is trellis;
dark energy lights up dark matter—stars disappear;
neurons re-enact dance evolution.

We live but once; a spin on off-bounce—
batter to bounce to batter
to squeeze to deliquesce.
Moon's backside views intrigue;
colour blends freeze time;
sky fireworks—nerve endings explode.

Live out your fantasies with unique courtesies;
you'll live on in form, informed and not deformed.

DOUBLE SPLASH

Sun smashes your mind
echoing early-morning brickbats.
Sweat-soaked clothes cling,
massage with every movement. Drops trickle,
tickle the back of your neck; you giggle.
Heck!   You wish morning exchanges changed.

Stream trail flashes vivid invite—cool fresh air.
Shrubs, trees in honour guard raise umbrellas;
flower fragrances float, feed scent sensors;
sunlight dribbles through, scribbles images that skip—
challenge to imagination.

You walk; your mind rescreens fiery focus of his eyes—
angry glare, solar flare. Untruth that spook him
you've not told. Morning exchanges brutal, strange—
your short attention span, his sloppiness, both arrows;
your neighbourhood service award, his promotion at
work, both hollowed. *Something else must be wrong;
we shouldn't lose our dreams we dreamed for so long.*

You peel your blouse, brassier, spread your arms;
gentle breeze wraps your upper body—cool silky sheet.
You breathe deeply, toss head back, slowly exhale.
It should be safe; it's working hours.

You take off your shoes, bottom wears;
tiptoe to the edge, toes in water.
Cold sensation races up your inners. Hands on hips,

you watch your image dance in time with
water ripples.

You wonder which of your hot spots is most sensual;
you recall his electrode fingers—white-fire tips that melt
resistance. You float off   re ve rie.

Smiles flash, reveal relished moments.   Your face,
muscles relaxed; the rest of your body in a million
micro massages, you nearly swoon.
Time stifled,   memory moments mesmerise.

Suddenly, that mellowed baritone from behind, "NICE,
I IMAGINED YOU'D BE HERE!" Startled, you jump.
Moments later, a splash; his body heat, water cold energise
your contact sensors—cold water sizzles.

Fervently your bodies range, rearrange your minds—
your love must live on . . .   Grass blades prostrate;
birds melodious; insects chirr; squirrels chirp on, hop,
flag tails.   Sun keels, shadows grow tails . . .

THE DREAM

It's free   You dream I dream
We all dream   Conscious
dreams we dream
To perch on lofty lofts
clad in baby blankets   To rise
to rupture ceilings high
To gain name that nods
heads through time
Trophy counts manage moments

Winged seeds dream too   Drift free on
high and low tides
Destination anyone's guess
Float wager HOPE to land
on fertile patch

Some dreams freewheel
Subconscious detached
make-believe   I do those too

Sometimes dramatic
I save my bully's life

At times traumatic
My gun jams in fierce firefight

Sometimes romantic
My love and I in Love Nirvana

At times psychotic
I fall into pit full of snakes

Sometimes epileptic
The shakes shunt sleep all night long

At times therapeutic
Overdue rent worries walk away

Sometimes telepathic
WAKE UP my twin shouts from Australia
I jerk up in cold Siberia
Smoke from hallway next room
Seeps into my bedroom

I dream the inimitable Mandela
The Madiba
The mighty MLK in collar
The JFK on country
And dandy Gandhi on hungry humanity

There's a dream I can't escape   Nectar
that draws bees away from me to their famed
duty   Soft pillow that cushions my falls
Scented sponge for my sweat my tears
Titanium screens for my lowly acts
Floaters that lift my moribund moods
Plaster for my wounds   Tenderiser that tames my
fiery furies   Tinder that fervours my
flames my flashes   That fast fastener for my
egos   That feast for my muse   Well-being in a
sanctuary well assured   Taut cords that position my
exuberance

You're that dream I can't escape at every blink
Blinks turned winks turned sleep
We'll pair to fit the bill without a slack
We'll not everything to each other be
Many fits will carry merry two-way cheers
I must burn taller to match your flame
I will I swear I will

I'll love you until my lungs launch your name no more
Flares quench fast ours will brightly glow through time
Partner me past our gaits slow our frames bowed
We'll still needle cuddle fondle and trundle dreams
In all of me I ask
Partner me with all your blank cheques

For Welugewe & Mulubwa,
my daughter & her husband,
(THE LEADING BRACE).

CLIMB REVIEWS

Acting fame, in part, from hunts;
wannabes pursue podium mounts.
Every so often, that couch
plays and pays so much.
Later famous curse the pigs' grunts.

BURNED-IN PROCESSES

"Events naturally vent advent of
wisdom," you often hear.
Listeners' ears flare, minds workout,
brows crease. Eyes focus far, heads tilt.
You hold hands to assure.

Singed infant tea-brewer invites adults
when next kettle whistles. Innocent infant,
alien to world—sensors quick-fill memory
chips; pixels pattern out on canvas, images
emerge, stamp mind.

EARLY MYOPIA

I feel I can do or be anything
in my time and enabling prime.
Good reason will not be in prison;
prison forgives not a bad reason.

In my time and enabling prime,
prison precincts are clear, not near;
prison forgives not a bad reason.
We all have targets in tiers, so clear.

Prison precincts are clear, not near.
Boundless HOPE maroons fear.
We all have targets in tiers, so clear;
abundance heaps everywhere.

Boundless HOPE maroons fear.
Only self carries barriers;
abundance heaps everywhere,
choices galore—every dip, rise, or turn.

Only self carries barriers
in age to belong and be so sung.
Choices galore—every dip, rise, or turn;
adoration rations, short and long.

In age to belong and be so sung—
pleasurable consumption, only option;
adoration rations, short and long;
future features praises, liberty.

Pleasurable consumption, only option,
no one bucks trend or harbours doubt;
future features praises, liberty.
Vast walls of grand goals rise.

No one bucks trend or harbours doubt;
before crucial milestone, puberty,
vast walls of grand goals rise.
In time, many tracks veer, tear apart.

Around crucial milestone, puberty,
hints, qualifiers introduce reality.
Many tracks start to veer, tear apart—
multi pressures without multi vents.

Hints, qualifiers introduce reality.
Good and bad reasons both in prison
from multi pressures less multi vents.
Do I still feel I can do or be anything?

RISE

For you, at last,
an ovation; spot-on icon
you are rightly called. Recall
and reflect on those pedestalled
who still have more of the answers—
the stars, the mega-stars, and the masters.

POETRY CLASS WINDS

Poetry, poetry, poetry . . .

Language of languages—layered than
allium buds or tamer cabbage lettuce;
conversation expansion; mini-universe;
definition, passion, action, commentary;
kaleidoscope of life: wind, water, wear, waste;
emotion infraction, confrontation commotion,
decompression compassion, nurturing nature;
pinhole to taut balloon; soporific to workaholic
nerves;   sanity in chaos;   tether to
paranormal,   rapture,   salvation!
In parallels, the unhinged re-hinge.

Poetry, poetry, poetry . . .

Production labour rewards, tickling wages—
quiet bomb; hot knife hiss in lard; meanings to
chords and clatter; love kisses of doves.

A high without the puncture
A high without the tincture
A high without alveolar rupture
A high without synaptic torture.

Interpreter of workouts, blind vision, mute shouts.
Jury on bouts: soul, mind, body, outlook. Ramrod to
neurotransmitters; timeless stills that mutter backstories.
Victor, but never bloody.

Poetry, poetry, poetry . . .

Themes tweak in, wink welcome;
abstraction extraction, mutation construction.
Telescope on future. Craft-tools' stashes—hush-hush fluid,
precious emitters piled landfill-like for the
bumps, dips: prompters, tips, reminders on which
broad road zigzags, climbs.

Protégés at the mountain base, amazed,
fixated to the peak—difficult climb;
loose overhangs, rarefied air.

Anointed masters boom from the top—staccatos,
tremolos, reverberations, echoes.

Weal over woe in slow full soak: HOPE homes.

Poetry, poetry, poetry . . .

Is there more to say or gain?
        Em . . . Count fine sand grains—absolutely!

What else is must-know, you silent volcano?
        Language musicality less syntax rascality.
        Off formalism, format out-fliers fly,
        scramble neurons of Scrabble player champions.
        A coup against beauty cooped-up—haste, waste.
        Believe—mastering mounted masters upheaves.

You cannot be buried; you cannot but live on,
eternal life various, gorgeous.

Poetry, oh, poetry!

Appreciated:
University of Iowa, USA,
IWP MOOC 2015 Poetry Class.

HAIKU FLAVOURED HOOTS

BUSH FIRES
(Linked haiku)

Winds strip off dead leaves;
Trunks' branches—multi-forked horns,
thirsty antennas.

Air sucks up moisture—
forked horns emaciate brittle,
wave for thirst-quencher.

Thirst-quencher is rain.
At times, arrives with lightning;
no rains at Forked Horns.

Lightning on two stilts—
one wet, other fiery,
plants either or both.

Stilts' choice is built up;
atmospherics, particles
thumb the scale of choice.

Scale, these days, ups counts
of fiery stilts' footprints.
All footprints enlarge.

Forked horns are ash heaps,
so are all neighbours recast.
That's how footprints grow.

Footprints, footprints stamped;
acres shed green turn black-grey.
Vision-tunnels pan.

Wildlife scurry, starve;
the more unfortunate die.
How comes this blaze trend?

DEEDS

Rainfall rills, high winds,
transport some species starters.
Floras fall to acts.

MARBLED TIPS
(Linked haiku)

Race to space teaches.
Smoke billows, white jet lifts load;
Earth in atmosphere.

Atmosphere protects;
cosmic rays rule Universe,
but Earth in blankets—

Magnetic blanket;
atmosphere roughs up stray rays
that all as well hurt.

Shaded Earth breeds life;
intelligent life—shepherds.
Earth's blankets, premium.

On blanketed Earth,
all resources congregate;
results shame debates.

□   □   □

ONWARD

Agreed not decreed
is people's willed way forward.
Big blob is not rain.

GROWERS

People's opinions
perform democracy rites;
tall trees spindle plants.

ACCORD

Leader becomes grace;
when led, happily apace.
Hen fends for her chicks.

RELIEF

Dictator trades fear;
tainted halos backlight grins.
Thunderstorms recede.

UNDERCURRENTS

Columbus shakes hands;
Native Americans soul.
Humankind sets sail.

DOCTRINE

Violence blazes
when diplomacy throttles;
rains quench bush fire.

NOISE

Word not matched by deed—
dog barks, burglar raids pantry.
Morning breakfast slim.

BOOMERANG

When politics traps
economy, society's
volcanoes erupt.

SMOKESCREEN

Their hands on the stove,
politicians vacillate,
first eat fresh-baked goods.

◻ ◻ ◻

TRADEMARK

Theory and practice,
symbiotic Siamese double;
farm yields grade farmer.

REPLICA

Examples teach best;
cubs hunt with adult lions.
Forest guide leads hike.

OUTFLOW

Writer on blank page
gushes or freezes on preps;
nimbus clouds bring rain.

RECONNAISSANCE

Vendor wears out shoes,
firecrackers announce show;
lightning leads thunder.

CAVEATS

Dam water level
sizes irrigation reach;
tributaries feed dam.

COMPULSION

Overgrown farm spread—
farmer on gamblers' circuit.
Harvest barns empty.

REBUKE

Farmer's scale faulty,
futures buyers scurry off;
farm trade forecloses.

DEPLETION

Gifted footballer
shuns practice, healthful habits;
drought shames rainmaker.

FUME

Dead fish on counter,
kitchen stinks worse every day;
plumber charges more.

OUTCOMES

Mocked-up scarcity
recasts banquets mob affairs;
starved herd rush fodder.

MOTIVATION

Hero-soldier dares,
compulsive revenge armours;
youngster shoots rapist.

DEALS

Give-and-take habit
shelters relationships well.
Good farm hands cost more.

RETHINK

Daily rush to pile
crowns, jewels, structures so overt;
coffin space so small.

◻ ◻ ◻

SANCTION

Rights at birth are won,
wayward actions waylay rights;
blaze and rain tussle.

LAYERS

Core values backbone,
peripheral values flesh out;
sweat floats off make-up.

JUSTICE

Honour honours well
as rules rule competition;
drug cheats lose medals.

ATTRITION

Injustice is sly;
bears aftermaths—tears and guilt;
piled silt diverts stream.

INVESTMENT
Yes, gratitude is
fortitude to attitude;
bonus boosts morale.

ADVOCATES

True friends let you dwell
and swell true in your true self.
Motorists love sleet!

DISTINGUISHED

Anything special,
more so, the fewer partake;
twins come not often.

NUNNERY

Collective wardrobe
assents most personal requests;
windbreaks shelter homes.

DISTILLATES

Information leaps,
knowledge-grip slips then judders;
snow piles melt in spring.

EXPEDITER

"Don't know" is excuse,
picks seasons then abuses;
knowledge is sound sleep.

PATHWAY

For rise above noise,
performance is trailblazer;
deep roots find moisture.

SPLASH

Help to others comes
from self-love in overflow;
activists steer HOPE.

ILLUSION

Water flea on back,
floats near bridge, shouts, "Lift the Bridge!"
Massive ego dupes.

◘ ◘ ◘

REGRESSION

Memory mends memory
bends; adolescents wither,
hollow—Howl Prison.

RETURNS

Law and order, fair;
community helps police.
Street gangs seek self-worth.

STAKE

If truth puts you in
rain-soaked doghouse, persist on;
eclipsed sun comes out.

PRESUMPTION

City trumps village;
below glitter tales abound.
Summer breeds microbes.

PENALTY

Jetting with the sun,
day or night gains fake hours;
body clocks holler.

DISCREDIT

Orphanage lacks food,
admin staff steal donations;
whiteout strips landscape.

SLIPUP

Lookout man dozes,
early fall night masks movements;
platoon is routed.

◻ ◻ ◻

BIAS

Racism lives on—
flawed humanity wavers;
corn stalk heights vary.

FANTASY

Racist races self
towards elusive top class;
untrained climber falls.

OVERLOAD

Hard-set racist is
furnace that belches blood jets;
deep-frozen steel cracks.

IMMATURITY

Xenophobe reaps free,
hoards harvest, adores diapers;
shaded leaves pastel.

DEVALUATION

Call him enough names;
his self-confidence will go.
Snowflakes rise to sky!

SPOILER

Wily chauvinist's
innuendos are killjoys;
woodworms bore all year.

SKUNK

Prejudiced offhand
snipe is a fart that stinks long.
Clean snow crystals glow.

□ □ □

AUTHORITY

Sheltered hot drug lords
entangle, maintain fast friends;
winds boost dust storms.

FACILITATION

Supply-demand chains
connive, keep drug use afloat;
slope speeds up wheel roll.

CARNIVAL

Pharmacies looted,
pharmaceuticals unpacked;
town floats through seasons.

ABORTION

"Moodies" brands explode.
To target cradles bothers;
spring sprouts need blanket.

INCEST

Synapses astray,
mother daughter are sisters;
adrift monsoon strays.

DYSFUNCTION

Neurons dance crazy—
"Ice-in-veins" taps, kills mother;
garbage backs up stream.

GRADUALISM

Fostered drug abuse
is homicide in vile stealth;
rainfall carves gullies.

FRACTURES

Drug abuse—no ruse,
subbase slacks, foundation cracks;
sinkhole swallows town.

WAYLAID

Expecting the bombs?
drugs' kills are already on;
nudes take winter hike.

□ □ □

UPSHOTS

Conscience is weighty;
Africa's past empowers.
Ridges hold rainfall.

CAPER

Voters vote, old young—
certain system change will be.
King reigns until death.

REVERSAL

Stashing funds afar
diminishes growth at home;
rain melts sugar stack.

PERFIDY

No-borders doctors
wing in, wipe tears all seasons.
Sick leaders fly out.

OUTCLASSED

Thunder flashes, rains,
mild winds cause power failures?
Astronauts spacewalk.

ENERGISER

Rhyme, rhythm, and pace,
Africa explodes leisure;
fireworks draw gaze.

RESPITE

Africa's pathways
her hero-nations will build;
rescuers tunnel.

BELLWETHER

Oh hail Nigeria!
Spring Africa's governance;
daylight follows night.

VOLTE-FACE

Africa disclaimed;
will seasons the same acclaim?
Spring restocks wardrobe.

ENRICHER

Everyone needs love,
dual carriageways raise traffic;
poor soil crops harvest.

GEYSER

Love springs from within,
self-worth, self-love power love;
hot spring carries heat.

RISK

Absence of true love—
wrecked-compass Pacific sail;
sea storms sink small boats.

DURABILITY

Kicks and treats done gone;
pure love pairs core-values pairs.
Rain shows up oil spill.

DASH

Physicals of love
only transient sensations;
snowflakes flash off fast.

BOUNCE

Speed him on, speed her
some fun; rickety bed splits—
doctors do splinters.

FREEZER

Libido puckers,
winter chill chills sensation;
expletives clutter.

SCUM

Hungry baby screams,
adults provide baby food.
Paedophile, stone deaf.

SWINE

When sex is service
on call, sexist imposes;
flood ebb leaves dung slush.

FLIPSIDES

Love and hate border,
daily emotions flavoured;
Daytime seams nighttime.

PROSE POEMS PING

WRONG MUSIC

To you, the clock crawls and blinks are hours on any Sunday
mother favours your favourite legume. Super pods, ellipsoid,
lime-green fresh and ash-brown dried; vast nitrogen-fixation
champion. Everyone knows your penchant; you gorge
on Sunday—stuffed bulk bag. Your alimentary canal,
its embedded neurons, take over for some hours on
hard labour obligations. All night and morning, you,
a charged balloon, resists lift off. Family leaves, you,
in bathroom Monday morning. Very late lunch at pet
neighbourhood diner with your kind of music. As you enter,
a cherished tune creates acoustic tremors. Heavy riffs
from bass guitars, bass drums led by snares, huge
talking drums, and blaring horns—heartbeat-trippers,
guts-shakers. You arrive to smiles; everybody knows
everyone. As you eat, the urge to deflate, but you are too
hungry to leave food for the toilet. You decide to unlock
relief in spurts that correspond to heaviest beats. After two
minutes, you look up. Everyone is scoffing at you,
pointing, cursing; shuffling away. You look around more,
similar reactions; cords to your earphones you plugged
your ears with caress your neck. "UL-LA-LAH!   Deep
sinkhole, why are you holed up elsewhere so far from here
and me?" you mutter, your sight tunnel avoids faces.

IN A CROWD YET ALONE

The entrapment by loneliness is the encampment of desires on wings—reasonable desires, questionable desires, even treasonable desires. Prism's density referees its diffraction games. A leap from Antarctica onto the heart of Africa burns-in temperature rise—mushroom-sprouter Mother Continent. Bloodline and tasers-and-tranquilisers architecture, direct, preview, and review our worldviews of the expansive prefecture.

From the rural-rural out there, Wakawaka springs onto the high stage in quite an age—perpetual motion everywhere chases time; noise has no notion of sleep; daylight only dims lightbulbs; thumps, glides, and slides flash by—details lie lonely. Wakawaka chins-up, does his dances of his native songs. His audience splinters—some pairs of palms slap each other, some eyeballs strain their tethers, some lungs contract in spurts, and some limbs retract. However, his nightmare cage is the underground train hub.

Without sky's reflections, evenly staggered lightbulbs' clusters replace sun and sky, and squash, but super empower vision. He observes ants in their busy routes with edible crumbs as nodes. The air is dense and is regularly pistoned to trip the rhythms of lungs. Compressed beehives of people jostle; many bounce off others, but move on. On the platforms and in the trains, practised apology-tokens for minor infractions post up privacy tents. Any prattle that spies further, no matter intent, is repelled by the tents. On long straightaways, silence bears down like a dense, dark raincloud. The knock-offs of rail joints by the wheels, which do not screech or whistle, are loud and echoed. Wakawaka imagines that dialogues happen through button taps that send invisible, silent signals to portable screens.

He often loosens the choke. With his wide-open eyes without steady focus, he relaxes his body, his mind performs to punctuate on prompts: *That clean-cut young man standing to my right, is his next stop a floral shop or a shiny desktop . . .? The lady who ignores her children—eyes half-closed; veins bead the sides of her face; lips protrude as if reaching for a kiss, but who would fearlessly intrude to kiss her? She holds on so tight to the hand bars over the seatbacks and stands as if she pushes the train. Did she just have a fight with teachers or is she going to one elsewhere . . .? The bones-out, middle-aged man seated over there, he pigs from his brown paper bag and obliviously sucks his straw that flutes loud for washdown; does he have family meals on a dining table or what kinds of dinners is he invited to . . .? The young man in front of me with eyes closed and no earphones on, his body gyrates. His upper body sways from side to side, while his lower section thrusts back and forth in slow motion. On occasions, his face lights up, then fades into creased cheeks, his gritted teeth visible. Em, will I be soon sprayed with his passion fluid . . .? That one with face full of hair—eyes shaded by eyebrows that eyelashes lash; pointy nose juts out like a bushy, fruit-vine stake; mouth anchors moustache and beard that pats his navel. He must spend hours before the mirror as the clipper mows down strands that stray. The rest of his body must be extra-insulated; good for the nasty, cold weather. If I took him home, though, he would run around naked; emm hunters would be pre-briefed, of course. But, but, in a hand-to-hand combat, whom would his beard favour . . .? My goodness! Look at that piece of nature's perfect artwork. Every portion in streamlined proportion; her sculptured, fulgent face beams appeal. Her every movement rushes the rushes of special moments. Statues' knees must buckle in dips to celebrate her beauty. Me, too. I bet my mattress would gladly wrap her up and push me onto an elevation that is easily breached. Oh-oh, Careful boy! Her armed tribesmen could charge in protest.   Strangely, though,   very few notice her; most act as if they were her co-tenants.   The next time I see her, I must man up and speak to her; oh-no, my Ebony Charm will surely protest, even throw intercontinental, laser-guided, and fire-tipped lances. If she does, I believe I will catch the fire first . . . In this coach, as in others on this train, many invisible privacy tents materialise into newspapers, magazines, books that shield faces. Small screens suck up attention. Everybody on their own until, perhaps, thunderbolt strikes shock-out hearts . . . Oh well,   I guess we are, in some ways, derivatives from our native climates.*

At the super-lonely moments, Wakawaka copes further—he closes his eyes; his mind telescopes; he transposes himself.

BURIED ROOTS

What mound to hoe down so community can grow?
Elders' council dutifully ponder—that's no wonder.
From time, that's been pathfinder without broadcast
primes. Strange-skinned foragers gazed, gauged, left
amazed, but vow to daze.

Elders postpone deliberation for liberation of ideas to
hone. Every domain they excite as right, but ears they
post for them to roam. Without threat or flattery,
daughters' group, mothers' group, age-grade groups,
many men's groups, kindred groups, functional and
outpost groups all bring condiments for the soup.

Of the people, by the people, and for the people
eclectic mantras, nearly electric, now screen the sun.
Rays that escape acquaint and paint in vivid colours—
Intellectual property rights' horrors that leave many livid,
escaped rays cast as brittle and fickle in their trickle.

RED IMAGES FLASH

Empowering or cowering, human propensities; what realities
they all set off streaming—oh LORD!

Sunlight screens, concrete slabs over gutters, concrete pavements,
and surface tamping and asphalt topping for traffic, but the earthworm
still aerates the soil, and the winged seed still floats and floats,
still dances to wind's rhythms, and still lands on fertile patch.

The vast and dense thicket or barren terrain offers few invites.
Farther afield though, it's more muddy waters than impenetrable swamp,
but the mud romps and massages the feet. Malaria or filarial, or both,
or the more unknowns are ardently acerbic—few or no
resident permits to intruder-foragers. Red-hot imperialism's umbrage—
trending in syllogism—is purchase of rich heritage acreage and precincts.

The wild vault from barbarity to decadence, which left in-between civilisation
vacated, tickles Oscar Wilde. Death and usefulness coalesce, when the former
validates the latter. Shackled and abused bodies offer incarceration to the mind
and spirit for the incubation of hysteria, squander mania, amnesia,
and volcanoes.
So much ever so glittery or so schmaltzy, yet so ersatz in "Nirvana".

The rattler rattles before the battle. Nighttime surprises the beaver of note,
and that beaver endures eternity before sunrise. Deranged rooster, in contrast,
robs the roost. Massively manipulative queen queans away commanders,
comrades, colleagues, and friends from the king. Cougars cull comfortably
in practised packs. Cats keep rats, presumably as pets. Busy liberators have
long worked to show, tell, sing, and shout, "The choice of voice and the voice
of choice determine the poise of the trigger. Drop the gag and frolic in the gig.

Orchestrate enduring symphonies in durable harmonies in their numbers to serenade the Universe. Drain the brain to blend the trends."

Sun rises, peers, pans, sets, but folds up the days' summaries.
The ORACLE holds vigil for salvation days.

FLÂNEUR

Paulina prowls, pries, any guise. Hopefully, she's not a
secrets-merchandiser. You never know: the deep fry.
Risky business, but she's wise, always the prize without uneasiness.
Daggers drawn, guns cocked, missiles poised, exclusion enclaves encoded;
the vulnerable soft underbellies—individual privacy and state secrets.
Paulina trundles ontology, cosmology, and epistemology without abuse,
but to confuse. Some pay for others' guts disgustingly expelled,
even as they decay and stink. Making money is such a magnet.
Metaphysics, in its phases, is eternally cerebral, elusive in abstraction,
but sometimes, decorative. Dark nights provide cover for
mugger, burglar, or smuggler. The lure of others' intentions,
the lure of a-step-ahead bids turns boundaries between individuals,
boundaries between the individual and state, and boundaries
between states, elastomeric. Atmospheric challenges task pilots
on flightpath changes. Super egos, fanned by usurper ethos,
burgeon on to cudgel breakers, breakers against intrusions,
intrusions into individual privacy, or intrusions into state secrets,
code-named "State Security." Lances feign, thrust, and rejoin
in the free-roll, free-flow, nerves-relaxer repartee; you glide
along on the merry-ride party. She throws in a piggy-backer,
"My Tommy is late home every night; buddies and bars. Then,
the stench of a brewery that wobbles and talks. What time
did your hubby come home last night?" Not to make your voice
vociferous, not to parade your prickliness, not to set boundaries,
you softly home in, "Is something wrong at home?"

THEMES AND SCHEMES

Always a cheer—bright-eyed, full-of-questions children in class, hands in the air,
vie for the prize. Nothing crass, only spry fascination and dalliance with
education, while seeking brilliance and *future connections.* The IC,
NO; the steam engine, NO; the IC engine, NO; the transistor,
NO; the microscope, NO; the telescope, NO; the radio,
NO; the rocket, NO; the computer, NO!
The WHEEL,
the WHEEL—the PRIZE; the utmost invention in humankind's rise;
the invention
that first assailed gristle and muscle wear and tear; the invention that
exploded
production and consumption; the invention that positions
launchers—rockets,
missiles, grenades, heavy ammo, other WMDs, and access to
knowledge;
the invention whose concepts, precepts, and uses are ubiquitous,
persistent; the invention that wheels dreams,
themes, and schemes forward.

Themes and schemes—the former often camouflages
the latter—come in many shapes and drapes.

You and your school cricket teammates wheel into a plantains zone
for a match,
a must-win match. Plantains, loaded with iron and more sugar when ripe,
are a favourite. Your hosts ensure your outsized breakfast and lunch
are heavily plantains-based. On the pitch, your team occasionally
impart increased momentum on the ball, but your dives for

the ball, when you field, catch air; the balls career to
boundary. Plantains tipped an otherwise even
contest away from your team. You all
need to forget.

More frequently these days, when you want to leave for work, you
have a flat tyre.
Your trusted vulcaniser only finds damaged valves. Puzzle pulverises you—
you ponder long, deep, and proper. _"Every previous evening, instead of
a walk, I drove around the block with my Alsatian dog. Routine
calls for walk, not a ride around the block. **Thank goodness,
it's only the dog and not my son, Doug!"**_

Astonished warlord wants to protect his reputation. Untenable
casualties and defeat
loom—some enemy fighters, civilians, drop from poisoned wells and
produce.
The skirmish is short; he wins, but both sides' many wounded
wrestle with pain.

Nightmares. Visions. Traumas. Decorated wounded veteran from
multiple services
cannot sleep or socialise. "I emptied many magazines, yet they kept
coming;
they kept coming; they kept . . ." The monologues, the duologues,
the multi-directional monologues with virtual reality
company gradually escape rarity.

Utility of painkillers ranges—analgesic and psychedelic effects overtip.
Endorphin production shuts down; opiate receptors go on furlough;
unpredictability becomes reality, but not enough reality about
the lean of the schemes for "THE APOCALYPSE".

SPECIES' INDOLENCE

Assess, yet the Anthropocene Era, the outgrowth within a human lifetime, the summation of "acceleration," etches the Planet. Fabled tortoise retracts head and limbs into its shell from clamour, but remains visible, with its protection only as good as its shell is tamper-proof armour, no matter how good the shell mortise. The rituals every four, five, or six years, or thereabout, see, in most power epicentres, with power defined variously, the public airing of dirty linens with from fetid green to blood-red stains, but the appearance of deliverance is the point. The tenet matter though, the real hot matter; yes, the matter burning brightly on all burners is RIGHTS.

Rights, yes, RIGHTS! The matter of the rights transient trustees have over the subject of their trusteeship tips the scale first. The beehive issues, disturbed at great peril, are the rights transient trustees have over themselves, collectively or as individuals.

Hunter-gatherer turns innovator-inventor; the ladder acquires punishing rungs.

"Acceleration", "acceleration"—production, consumption—the latter riding and whipping the former to exert more, pace up the race to brace the tape in a reckless race, even as human biomass spikes to the skies. Millennia, millions, or even billions of years hence, stratigraphic enquirers of whatever form are affronted: Littering clutter of lithospheric signatures—blinking artificial radionuclides; carbon-laden particles; recalcitrant repositories of artificial artefacts, Anthrosols and Technosols, or together, Technofossils; geomorphology

apologies; flexed sedimentary fluxes; migrant and other species rewired, mired,

marooned, or doomed; altered aquifers altered their domains and qualities.

Holocene and Anthropocene dovetail, but tussle on the point of which one
came first and when to claim more assay, they say.

At that geologic timeline, the enquirers reason that the impact of
"acceleration"
eyeballs that of a huge asteroid hit. Cascades of charades upgrade or
degrade
not a single grading, but only seed more long-term upbraiding.

On the so-far unique Planet, issues trend and bend common-destiny
views,
while imagination images and stages skin-colour, dominion, and
lifestyle divides.
Humanity all along smothered Mother Planet Earth with reverence,
gratitude,
and TLC (Tender Loving Care; not to be mistaken for the natural or
synthetic
cannabinol, THC), yet she spits back on humanity's face!

THESE TIMES

Hubris, hammers of hubris, manhood in prime; I should exude those
at this time. I dreamed of stethoscope-adorned neck. Extreme
violence intruded—I was scrubbed. No way to cope,
even with stethoscopes near. I now share
stories with close pals in our world;
I'll tell you some of them.

"'Belo! Belo!' women baited Paulo in Rio. 'The Flash,' after nifty
paces,
was set to spray blessings. His fascinating fire, Francisca, treaded fast
and frantic; she exploded in spit-fire Portuguese— 'That thick,
long snake shoving my tongue out? No way!' Paulo eased
into cold bath, after stroking the snake to spit;
he thus averted a blackout.

"Jimmoh's lineage competes in marrying early. This didn't bother
him; his twins did. At his wedding, he and his wife in late
teens, their eight grandparents sheltered themselves,
partied to their hearts' desires—imagined, vintage
shuffles. Upshots! His paternal grandfather, his
wife's maternal grandmother fell in love,
later divorced partners, married—time
still ahead. If they have children, their
twins would call the children what?

"Bubbly Becky, smiles and giggles alive,
was 8, brother Phil, 10, when father, 38, died.
Phil daily imaged father more, tapped warp speed.
Becky mended fastest; mother, her concern. Unknown to her,

mother and Phil used marijuana, then hard drugs. Many years on,
mother delivers a baby boy, shadow of father, Phil's features engraved.
Explosions—three homicides, one suicide—mother sprawled, gun in hand.

"Busy inventor Ben, absently, when told his assistant, mechanic, and his
friend were romping his wife, "Eh   em   it's okay;   there's   no
metre   or count to countdown.   Uhm   as long as   I don't
feel like   a shunted train that freewheels   back and forth
in the tunnel,   or having   to endure   a stink bomb,
it's okay". Months on, Ben rushes home with a secret
weapon prototype to show his wife who, locked in
lust with his friend, became first test target
of new invention. A triple.

"Outrage seeks revenge—often, after hearing my friends' stories,
I manage out a pensive rejoinder, flaccid like, 'I frequently
hear a strange man and woman sprinkled with grey hairs,
hundreds of miles apart now, speculate on what
I could have been doing for myself or them.
I was a healthy robust girl about to stake
strong claims and stands. They knew.
Not everything though.'"

FOUR-DAY WEEK

Cultural vortex, the cerebral cortex for stream-of-awareness
spin-offs, interior monologues—all parallel with popular power
prisms. From where its "locus standi"? I profess, it's "sui generis"
here; four days—NKWO, EKE, OLIO, and AFOR—make the week;
no day is bleak and a lot impress. The elder is pivot point. Every day is
market day in one community or the other in the cluster. Friends call me
"Dave the Brave," a throwback—the Goliath yack. Jimmy and Wong,
my friends, and I get lucky. Our plea, a week in elder's home, is not
wonky. Cultural nuances to apprehend and log (databanks may pay;
revered explorers did their bits for more than tips; we shouldn't stray).
Much to crave out or jimmy into without doing outright wrong.
Elder Anachunam, centenarian, slim and trim, average height, agility and
alertness amazement, drips wisdom, wisdom as tonic, wisdom as sedative,
wisdom as firearm, wisdom as armour, wisdom in measured word-
packs that intermittently tumble out from his creased lips. Drooping
eyelids, is he
napping or mapping?

We arrive NKWO midmorning. Minutes later, a handful of young men
arrive. Ambience is protocol and decorum on floatation, no matter the
occasion. Every structure is built with culture and tradition—
blocks and mortar in personification; reverence, as paint, soaks through.
The men sit. The one with face contorted is most ready to fight; the
one with
legs wagging is most ready to fight; the one with puckered lips is most
ready
to fight; the one whose arms restrain each other over his chest is most
ready
to fight; the one with eyes ablaze and feet tapping is most ready to fight;

the one whose shoulder muscles twitch and heels stomp is most ready
to fight,
perhaps, it's him—the husband. Everyone stands. Elder Anachunam
comes in, sits. Kernels of complaint: a well-to-do fellow in a
neighbouring community has been bunking the leader's wife
and honking about it to all ears within earshot. Elder to intervene
or else—soldier-hunter ants; incisors cutting out transportable bits of the
earthworm, the price on the day the straying worm has to pay.
Elder sits up from backrest, eyes wide open. He slowly fathoms faces,
including ours, without a blink. My friends and I shrink. He focuses on
husband, "Emm   Did I miss   a rape   complaint?   Eh   Are your
ceiling paint colours   psychedelic enough   for your wife?"
Heads bow; emotions earn fast demotions. My friends' eyes and mine in
instant radar-lock on: *Poor lady, man in the dock, some mess; lots of luck!*

EKE: Kindred heads request a ruling. Primary school project,
projected for growth and enhancement, requires some land,
but kindred landowners demand rattling exclusives—automatic
admissions, no fees, no levies, staff placements, other caveats.
Elder Anachunam leans forward, eyes in rare glare, "You all are
  too young. I was only a boy then. Some time ago,
  some decades ago, produce in these our parts rotted;
  lack of buyers—disastrous consequences. Services
from government were slow or absent. Then, government
built the dual carriage road that now connects these our parts
  to the state capital and to the rest of the world.
Guess what? Not a brass coin or a tuber of yam was
given to any of the landowners on whose land the road
sits. **Good day to you all.**"

OLIO: Constituent family heads of an extended family complain;
a particular nuclear family has a history of deviant behaviour.
A young man from the said family is causing earthquakes—

ascending serial outrages that shake foundations and cause severe
connection outages. They request permission to repost the harsh
past in extreme. Elder Anachunam, relaxed and amused,
beams and muses, "The long snake   begets not   a short offspring.
    Long or short,   snakes can be   dangerous.   Even snake
    charmers
    know this well.   Yet,   they house and train snakes;
    swell audiences   entertain them well.   And,
the snake moults—season changes,   new growth." As they leave,
emphatic lead speaker heaves, "Exile at home!"

AFOR: Elders' council in all day debates and discussions—
Directions: youth directions, adult directions, governance directions,
global directions, all directions supposed to direct peace, security,
and sustainable development, direct contrariness. The youths
in particular; ears plugged up with headphones, no longer listen to
or respect authority—so un-Afrikan. The Harmattan, they argue,
is causing chills, pain, and blowing out windowpanes. Trends
will truncate the future. Squinting Elder Anachunam, concern palpable,
deals doses, "You cannot stop   the wind   ***with your hands.***
    Grow or build   windbreaks.   They will slow   the winds
    and make them more peaceful.   While on all that,   ramp up
your thoughts about   fusillades—bullets, shrapnel, grenades,
    and analgesics,   and strange illnesses,   and strange
    bacteria, viruses;
    much abnormality these days.   Sometimes,   I think that
    laboratory
animal cages   are shaping mysteriously." He peers at my friends and me,
"Spread   the word!" We flinch and bow in reflex response.

Four-day weeks; not bad at all. They clip on fast, as
Elder Anachunam presides.

BIRTHDAY GREETINGS RESPONSE

Harmattan, hurricanes, snow blizzards, and sand storms
all have blown. Deep canyons, hot ovens, tropical sun,
and furnaces have all baked. Deep freezes have turned
exhaled breaths tiny hailstone puffs with ease. Earthquakes
and tremors have quaked. Self-sown seeds have grown.
Dry and steamy air have tested lungs. Birds have sung
their songs. Ladders have been magnetic with their rungs.
Step-towers have empowered then cower. Shaved right
and wrong have stung, some so strong. From hard nuts
to mushy tubers to soup suspensions, has been molar
markdown slide. Meal rations now include dentition portions.
Flush-spigots have donned squashed seal rings. Sounds that
shattered have remained to matter. Erstwhile sharp objects
have gained partners. Memory misshapen, mesmerises—
messages maintained, messed up, or missed, all capped time.
Memory has been mined more for treasures, body has lagged
mind more, with lapse of time. Stubborn chases of earlier
stripes have raised gripes of concern. Decision matrices
have grown complex, compel. Not to disrobe in public, sizes of
wardrobe items have been roped down. Silent documentaries for
private commentaries have rolled. Fears have speared,
tears and cheers have worked face wipes.

How does it feel to be seventy-seven? First, "seven" is lucky,
double "seven," double lucky. But to still stay alive and
understood to be for good in most neighbourhoods, you tiptoe,
hop-step and skip-and-jump on markers, as trackers, and tell
a tale or two: It's never too late to up the take to slow debate
and widen gate. Others' skirts, others' shirts, are best fits, but

peruse synonyms that often suffuse. A group's success against
formidable odds expresses the essence of apex human bond.
HOME HOPE, as you roam contacts, and take home enlarged
HOPE. Wisdom in the old is gold, not to be wasted in any hold.
Bottom-line distillate, which so many hate—it's a common
humanity, one destiny in the long view.
There's no review.

Thank you so much for your birthday good wishes, touches,
and for the punchy punch!
Love You Much.

About the Author

Hailing from Oyofo Oghe, Enugu state, Nigeria, novelist/poet Chukwuajalike C. Aningo studied mechanical engineering at University of Wisconsin as an ASPAU (African Scholarship Program of American Universities) Scholar. He variously served in projects on six continents as general manager technical, chief engineer, and other very "impressive" titles. In between setting production records, coaching a company soccer team, and launching his own engineering company, Aningo has published *The Nigerian Engineer by and after the Year 2000* (1997), *My Cry for Nigeria: A Challenge to Our Essence* (2011), first edition, and several articles and poems on engineering, social, and environmental developments.

Aningo believes that any artificial curtailment of the full expression of an individual's talent is the *first sin* against humanity.

Aningo's technical background gives a uniquely methodical perspective on the ways leadership, love, morality, and the struggles therein reveal the core of human nature. He writes that "Everyone is a library; each book, bestseller. /Tweak stories—how truly one we all are!" and that "we all come naked then go portfolio-less; /medical science ceaselessly choreographs alliance."

His political verses are scathingly patriotic, as a son demanding excellence from his beloved Mother Nigeria, and his haiku offer profound and comedic twists on matters of the heart, flesh, and mind. A range of emotions and challenges shout out from his prose poems. Overall language musicality gilds his poems.

Chuks Aningo currently resides in Enugu, Nigeria, where he enjoys growing fragrant flowers, tomatoes, okra, and others; listening to highlife, reggae, jazz; watching soccer, boxing, and American football; and pontificating with his dear wife and three adult children. He spends quality times with members of his Oyofo Oghe community's UCA (Umu-ogba Chukwuajalike Aningo) Age Grade he mentors as the traditional "Father" of the Age Grade.

Email: ccaningoboox@gmail.com
Blogsite: www.beamnaijadream.com

www.ingramcontent.com/pod-product-compliance
Lightning Source LLC
Chambersburg PA
CBHW021155020426
42331CB00003B/70